"FASCINATING, THOUGHTFUL
AND ENTERTAINING . . .
YOU DON'T HAVE TO BE A FATHER
TO ENJOY *FATHER FEELINGS*."

—Ezra Jack Keats, children's book author and illustrator

"Rare blend of sensitive, warm wisdom done with humor and a light touch. I strongly recommend this book for all parents."

—Dorothy C. Briggs,
author of *Your Child's Self-Esteem*

"A DELIGHTFUL LITTLE BOOK—warm and humorous . . . provides other fathers with a model of how a caring parent can develop intimate relationships with his children"

—Dr. Thomas Gordon,
author of *Parent Effectiveness Training*

"The humor and the care which he mixes so masterfully in the resolution of his fatherly trials add hope to all our fatherly (and motherly) strivings."          —Fred. M. "Mister" Rogers

# ELIOT A. DALEY

# FATHER FEELINGS

PUBLISHED BY POCKET BOOKS NEW YORK

**POCKET BOOKS**, a Simon & Schuster division of
**GULF & WESTERN CORPORATION**
1230 Avenue of the Americas, New York, N.Y. 10020

Copyright © 1977 by Eliot A. Daley

Published by arrangement with William Morrow & Company, Inc.,
Library of Congress Card Catalog Number: 77-22820

ISBN: 0-671-82271-3

First Pocket Books printing September, 1979

10  9  8  7  6  5  4  3  2  1

Trademarks registered in the United States and other countries.

Printed in the U.S.A.

FOR THOSE WHO HAVE HELPED ME FEEL—ESPECIALLY

ALISON

AND

SHANNON

AND

JAD,

OF COURSE

# FOREWORD

I SUPPOSE IT IS RIGHT, IN A KINKY SORT OF WAY, FOR THE foreword to be the last thing the writer writes—but the first thing the reader reads. Since, at this point, I'm the only one of us who knows what lies before you, perhaps a word of orientation is in order.

In the more than a dozen years I have been a father, I have been stirred to every imaginable parental feeling —raised to ecstasy by my children's sensitivity and generosity, and ashamed by their greed and jealousy; encouraged by changing sex role expectations culturally, and astonished at the obstinacy of my own habits of mind; frustrated by my ineptitude in some parent-child interactions, and awestruck at the graceful forces which swept in to redeem others.

My hunch is that such stirrings of feeling, and the responses one makes to them, constitute most of what matters about human life. All the rest—all the going and coming, getting and spending, building and breaking and building again—are probably the lesser part, even though they apparently dominate our days.

So I determined to write of a year in the life of my own father feelings in order to raise them to proper stature in my own everyday life. By taking the time to identify them and write them out, I hoped, perhaps I could accord them the claim on my attention they deserve. And so I did.

That year's musings are before you. If it turns out that reading them evokes for you any hint of the human balance which writing them evoked for me, then I will be doubly gratified.

E.A.D.

*1976*

BECAUSE ALL OF WHAT FOLLOWS TOOK PLACE SOME *place*, it might help to know where that is.

Princeton, New Jersey, mostly.

We have lived here twice. And therein lies a modest tale—a "backgrounder," if you will—with which I begin this chronicle of a year in the life of a man who is glad to be a father.

# STAYING PUT

## *or*

## *STOP THE WHIRL, I WANT TO GET OFF*

IT'S DIFFERENT NOW. WE'RE SETTLED. BUT HALF A DOZEN years ago, we were still dues-paying members of the mobility generation.

If you had met me at a party and asked where I was from, there would have been a pause. Even though I had had a thousand chances to practice a ready response, I still never got it right. So, instead, there would have been a brief, earnest silence—just for a beat or two—while I imagined whether anything was likely to matter enough between us for me to really tell you.

To tell you where I was born (Boston), as opposed to where I went to kindergarten (Napa), as opposed to where I went to elementary school (Oakland), as opposed to where I went to high school and college (Fresno), as opposed to where I began my professional career, as opposed to where I continued it; all of these as distinct from where I might then have been living— until we moved again.

I would have known what you were asking, all right: Where is home?

But I couldn't have given you a straight answer. Like many in our generation, I had lived in a lot of places. But I was stagnant compared to Patti, my wife. Her family moved twenty times before she entered college. (No, her father was neither a military man nor a migrant agricultural worker—just an electrical engineer who worked for the same public utility company for his whole life, and went where they sent him. If I had graduated from college into the pit of the Depression, I suppose I might have displayed similar fealty to the powers who gave me work.)

IBM—"I've Been Moved," to their personnel—didn't invent the uprooted family. They just carried it to perfection.

Or ruination.

Our parents' generation may have sown the first seeds of mobility, but we have certainly been fertile and fruitful bearers of them, accepting frequent relocation as one of the givens of our time.

I was no different. Patti and I got married in the midst of our college friends and our families—and promptly moved away.

Doesn't everybody?

After all, we can always keep in touch. If we think to. Besides, "they say" it's good to put a little distance between newlyweds and the folks.

Good for what, was never quite clear. But everybody knew it must be good for something.

So we pushed on—two eager teachers (Patti in speech therapy and education of the deaf; I, masquerading in English) out to find a place of our own. We spent a couple of years in a charming coastal village near Santa

Barbara; made some warm friends there, too. Honey, you remember the . . . uh . . . oh, you know, the people with the twins. Name'll come to me in a minute.

But I wanted to learn more, enough to build a career on. So in 1963 we moved on, Patti now pregnant with Alison. Three years of study in theology and psychology in San Anselmo, California, lay ahead. It was only seven or eight hours' drive north of Santa Barbara, and we were sure we'd drive it often to see our old friends.

We did—but not often. And by the third Christmas we were content to exchange cards, ours now including pictures of Alison's new sister Shannon who was born in 1965.

We still exchange those cards.

Just like we exchange them with our San Anselmo friends, the ones we left behind when we went to Middlebury, Vermont, where I worked as a chaplain at the college. Just like we exchange them with our Middlebury friends, the ones we left behind when we moved to Princeton, where I worked as a minister, and where our son, Jad, was born in 1969. Just like we started to exchange them with our Princeton friends when we moved to Pittsburgh, where I began my work in television.

Stop.

Where in the world *was* I from?

And where would I have been from next?

Enough moving. Here we had just left one more set of friends we loved, and by whom we felt loved. The kind of people who not only sat in lonely late night hospital corridors together, haunted by the dark of a sickroom doorway, but friends who could fiercely accuse another of squandering their talents on an ill-chosen career.

*Those* kind of friends.

These were people who loved our children as much, in their own way, as we do. These were the people who shared the cautious joy of Patti's unexpected and obstetrically complicated third pregnancy—and then the burst of sheer joy at the safe arrival of our son, Jad.

These were people we wanted for lifelong friends. We did not want them, too, to slip into that netherworld of fading faces lost to us except once a year, at Christmastime, when a token is exchanged symbolizing the residue of a relationship.

So we decided to pack up our belongings, sell our Pittsburgh house, and move back to Princeton.

Explaining our decision to my colleagues was awkward, at best. "Yes, I still want to work with you. I love what we're doing together. How? Well, I'm going to commute each week. I'll do script writing in Princeton several days a week, then fly out here to handle my other responsibilities. No, I'll pay for the trips myself. I mean, *we* will—this is a family decision. No, we can't afford it. We simply can't afford not to.

"Just because it matters to us, that's why."

"You see, we want to have some lifelong friends, and if, over the years, it doesn't work out that way, it won't be because *we* kept skidding away."

And they understood.

So we came back, to stay.

And now I cannot imagine the circumstances under which we would move again. Not that every relationship here became petrified at a state of permanent perfection. Some friendships atrophied, as personalities and values and tastes evolved in different directions. Others have become richer than I could have dreamed, and they have made the bore and bother of a few hundred plane rides seem a paltry fare for admission to such caring.

I like knowing these people, and I like being known.

Being known is so different from being known about, being famous. For a long while I thought I wanted that, and it seemed fame would have warranted—probably required—a lot of mindless mobility.

But now I care less to be well known and more to be known *well* (and long) by friends who have pondered and supported the convolutions of my career, who have sensed the ebb and flow of fulfillment in our family, who have cared about the major and minor causes in which we are mutually joined, sometimes in cooperation and sometimes in opposition.

I know I have a place in their lives.

I know I have a place.

Period.

Perhaps all this is an overreaction, an idiosyncratic and anachronistic concern of someone who is discomfited by his inability to give a straight answer to a simple inquiry about where he's from. And it may not mean a thing to my children that their father threw out an anchor when the cultural tide started sucking us out of port once more.

But when somebody starts a conversation with *them* fifteen or twenty years from now by asking where they are from, there'll be no pause.

And think what a conversation piece *that* will be.

WITH THE NORMAL FRENZY OF CHRISTMASTIME PAST, I
have had a few minutes lately to work my way through
the accumulated cards, savoring as best I can some of
the fondest images and memories they evoke.

This year there are some fresh ones, from a time last
summer in Scotland when we met and studied with a
vibrant collection of new friends at St. Andrew's. (Even
though we have re-rooted permanently in Princeton, we
venture as often and as far as we are able—which is
never often or far enough to suit everybody.)

Wherever we are, however, my children are equally
likely to be the victims or beneficiaries of my fathering.
Sometimes both, as was demonstrated during a post-
St. Andrew's side trip to London.

# GUARDIAN ANGELS
# LOOK AFTER INEPT PARENTS
*or*

*FINDING OUT THAT THE DUMB THINGS
WE DO TO OUR KIDS CAN WORK OUT
ALL RIGHT—SOMETIMES*

I SUPPOSE IT COULD HAVE HAPPENED AT CONEY ISLAND or the Cheyenne Round-up or a mini-carnival temporarily clanking away at a shopping center parking lot. Guardian angels who look after children must be ubiquitous.

But the one who popped up to help five-year-old Jad was on duty at Battersea Park, an amusement area along the Thames River in London. All the standard accouterments are there—merry-go-round, bumper cars, go-carts, rows of stands where you could buy cotton candy and ice cream to juggle while pitching pennies onto, and on past, shallow glass saucers, leaving the giant furry panda bears, bored and unhuggable, forever consigned to the shelf of would-be prizes.

A huge roller coaster dominates the skyline of Battersea Park.

From the moment we arrived, it was like a magnet for Alison, ten, and Shannon, eight. They couldn't wait to get on it.

I could.

Roller coasters scare the wits out of me. Back when my teenage buddies were inventing new ways to defy death, standing up, no hands, forgetting the seat belt on the Big Dipper at Santa Cruz, I shuffled around amid the crowd below, wondering if my latest excuse for not going with them had really hidden my fear.

But bit by bit, I've been trying to outgrow some of those baseless tumors of reluctance, left over from days of old. Lately I've learned to love snakes, no less.

So I followed my daughters' lead, haltingly, taking Jad's hand as we made our way through the crowds toward the roller coaster. As I approached, I sized it up with concern worthy of an astronaut inspecting his space vehicle. Indeed, the state of the art of constructing roller coasters had advanced dramatically since my days twenty-five years ago in Santa Cruz. Here was no groaning, shuddering fretwork of aging timbers, split for inches around every rusting bolt.

The structure at Battersea Park was built like a base for the earth to rest upon. Marvelous iron beams, massive and gleamingly painted, bolted and welded and resolutely unified to steel the courage of the most fainthearted. I contentedly envisioned a squad of briskly competent British inspectors swarming over the structure each morning, before opening, satisfying themselves that each joint would outlast the Empire by centuries.

And anything that clean, I thought, had to be safe.

Alison and Shannon darted ahead and quickly returned with four tickets. *Four* tickets? I had forgotten about Jad, this little five-year-old whose hand I was holding for security.

No time to allow room for second thoughts.

"Come on, pal," I said reassuringly. "We're going to take a little ride together."

"I don't want to."

What's this? An expression of fear? Intolerable.

"Why, *sure* you do," I pressed. My resolve was firm. No son of *mine* was going to be afraid of any old roller coaster. I unloaded my whole arsenal of persuasion on him: cajoling, empathizing, challenging—the whole works. He did not want to go. He struggled. I won. I talked him into getting aboard the car with me.

It was the sorriest thing I ever did.

For the next eternity, or however long the car took to rocket its way around that horrific course, Jad Daley was petrified. Literally. Frozen with fear, unable to move, white as death.

He spoke only once, after a particularly punishing swoop brought us upward to an instant of pause before the next descent into terror.

"Why did you make me do this, Daddy?"

When the car finally stopped, we walked down the ramp together, shaken and shaking. We held hands. A bench was there, and we sat down. The girls were off on their second ride, I think.

Jad and I just sat. He said nothing. Minutes passed in slow motion. I put my arm around his shoulders. Then she came to me from out of the air and whispered to me what I should say.

"It's all right to cry now, Jad."

And he did.

God, what a beautiful thing, his crying. Flooding his tense body with relief, melting the rigid shell of bravado he thought I required, freeing him to be my little boy, afraid of the roller coaster and afraid of whatever possessed his father in luring him so far beyond his limits.

I cried too, of course.

It was a moment of beauty, our crying on that bench in Battersea Park. Jad was the only one who deserved it, but we shared it together.

FEBRUARY IS A CELEBRATED MONTH IN OUR HOUSEHOLD. It brings two anniversaries—one is of our wedding, and the other is of the birth of Alison, the child who first made us parents.

Anniversaries of any kind are a welcome occasion for looking back, as the rower does, marking both progress and bearings. And so we fell to talking, Patti and I, about becoming a couple, about becoming parents, about becoming a family. And I realized that it wasn't until our second child, Shannon, was born that I found out all that "becoming" didn't just happen.

It requires more learning—about myself—than is comfortable some of the time.

# THE CAREFREE DAYS
# OF CHILDHOOD
## *or*
## *FAILING TO REMEMBER IS*
## *FAILING TO RELATE*

I HAD A LOT OF THINGS ON MY MIND BACK IN THOSE SAN Anselmo days. A theological student in my mid-twenties, I struggled with exams and term papers and Greek and Hebrew during the hours I wasn't sweating out ways to stretch our meager family budget to cover the needs of myself, Patti, and Alison, who was now almost two. I earned a monthly salary of $150, and that had to cover everything.

Everything wasn't much.

We found a cottage to rent for $35 a month. Actually the cottage was a turn-of-the-century icehouse, situated on the grounds of a former hunting lodge. Its two hundred thirty square feet were cut into three tiny rooms. I do not believe the architect took carefully into consideration the fact that a nice young family like mine would inhabit the icehouse some day. Otherwise, he might not have made the ceiling only six feet high.

As fate would have it, my growing stopped at 5 feet, 11 inches, and Patti's at a good bit less than that. Our only problem was to develop good bobbing and weaving reflexes as we threaded our way among the several bare lightbulbs which protruded down from the ceiling. Like fragile stalactite grenades, they poised ready to implode against the forehead of a full-bladdered sleeper groping across the room in the dark. Some mornings we combed shards of Sylvania's best out of our hair.

Our friends did not come to call often. Children passing through the neighborhood did—mistaking this man's castle for a playhouse.

Right away, you can see there were more important things on my mind than Alison's psyche, even though Patti was well into the pregnancy which would produce Shannon.

In the two years since Alison had arrived and made me a father, I had taken extraordinary delight in her. Every milestone of progress was photographed and celebrated and telephoned to grandparents. Her exploits were duly exploited by her doting daddy, everywhere he went.

It never dawned on me that she was a *person* until a friend helped me see her that way.

He asked me how I had prepared Alison for the coming arrival of her sibling.

Prepared her?

Well, I supposed, we hadn't given it a lot of thought, although we did read all the right books about child development and knew theoretically that she'd have some feelings about the matter. At Patti's suggestion,

I had even taken pictures of Alison's nursing, to show her during the new baby's breast-feeding.

I imagine, my friend mused, that you've explained to her that she has been such a joy to you that you're having another baby because you wanted to multiply your pleasures, or some such rationale.

Exactly. But how did you know, I wondered.

Never mind about that, he went on. I get the distinct impression you underestimate the depth of her feelings.

Try this on for size: You have been down in the library until late, studying Greek exegesis. When you get home, Patti takes you by the hand and sits you down on the sofa. She fixes you a drink, and then snuggles next to you and tells you how great it is being married to you. How much you mean to her. What sublime pleasure you bring her. "In fact," she goes on, "you have been such a joy to me that I have decided to take on another man. Come on into the bedroom and meet Steve."

I got the picture. Suddenly a cute child became a person, capable of pain and loneliness and real hurt, as well as happy, burbling precociousness. And lapping right behind that new awareness was an older awareness, stale but still strong: much of my own fairly normal childhood was confusing and lonely and painful.

The waves of awareness persisted, and soon I had moved to well before the grammar school years, which had previously been the earliest memories available in any quantity, and lived again age five, and four. Then three.

Carefree childhood! Sure.

Slowly, as strangers emerging from a mist, figures approached and gradually became long-ago family and friends. Incidents recreated themselves, and I stood again in their midst and felt sudden showers of guilt and shame and dislike.

In the eighth grade, we were still oblique in our relationships with girls. Well, I was, anyhow. So when boys wore around their necks the scarf of the girl they were "liking," I went scarfless.

Until I remembered Sandra, who lived across the street.

A seventh grader, and a bit of a simpleton, she surely would have a scarf I could borrow. And she did.

"Whose scarf you wearing, Daley?" asked one of the guys.

"Wouldn't *you* like to know," I parried.

"I'll bet he bought it!" (General laughter.)

"No, I'll bet he decided to start liking Gail. Right, Daley?"

"I'll never squeal."

And so I wore a scarf which meant nothing to the giver, nothing to the wearer, and nothing to the beholders. Until one day dumb Sandra asked me to give it back—I forget why—right in front of everybody.

Unfortunately, I did not die.

That memory hurt. But less, for being remembered.

I worked my way back to fifth grade memories, to the time when Miss Head called me aside as I returned from recess.

"Is this your geography book, Eliot?" she asked in a measured, intense tone.

"Yes, ma'am."

"Then you are responsible for this, I presume."

The object of her presumption was the word "fuck" written large on the inside of the front cover.

I had not written it there, and looked around helplessly for someone to come forward to exonerate me.

All I found were averted glances. Everyone knew from the tone of Miss Head's voice, from her posture, that she was about to lower the boom on me.

Suddenly, I did not have a friend in the room. Andy Bewley, Fred Eby, Daniel Clifton, Kenneth Pinckney—all my buddies would have denied me.

And so, for some unfathomable reason, I was sent down the hall to Miss Batchelder's room. Why to Miss Batchelder and not to the principal? Beats me. I guess she was the most skilled humiliator on the teaching staff of the school.

She ordered me to the front of *her* fifth grade class, like a prisoner-of-war being marched on exhibition through city streets.

*"This,"* stubby, pugnacious Miss Batchelder said with a sneer toward me, "is the kind of student who is a disgrace to Montclair Grammar School."

I do not remember what she said after that. All I knew was that I was being humiliated, wrongfully, and that I could never look those students in the face again. I did not understand how any adult could be so mean. I still do not. But I do know, at least, that they sometimes are—and that my children sometimes experience them that way.

Earlier and earlier incidents crept forth, to be known anew by an older me, to be drained of their pain, to be put into perspective. And to remind me of the hidden life of my children.

—Staying home "sick" several days in the third grade, afraid to tell my suspicious mother that I was afraid to go to school where a big sixth grade kid called "Hemo" was waiting to beat me up.

—Taking a circuitous route home from school in the second grade, my jacket tied about my waist backwards,

like a loincloth, terrified that I would encounter someone I knew—someone who would surely know I had wet
my pants.

—Tumbling in pain and ignominy from my tricycle,
as a four-year-old, in front of a whole picniceful of on-
lookers for whose benefit and adulation I had come
charging down the bumpy hill in the first place.

I do not find it an easy or comfortable pastime to sit
around and conjure up images and recollections of my
earliest childhood. Yet I am convinced that it is worth
the time and effort and courage to do so. What I mean
is, our children are worth it. They may be the prime
beneficiaries.

In many ways, it's simpler for *us* to just let well
enough alone. We have long since come to some kind
of terms with those early days, recalling and celebrating
some moments, repressing and denying others. They
have established their power in our lives, nudging us
this way and that as we evolve through adulthood. Our
marriages, our pastimes, even our vocations respond to
the invisible sinews linking these days to those, as a
riderless horse still responds to the rhythmic slapping
of the reins on its neck.

But remembering is a gift we can give our children.
I am a different and better father when I am remembering.

On a generalized level, it tempers my complicity in a
cultural conspiracy. Because most of us have packed
away our painful memories of childhood and have
chosen to keep available for recall and display only the
better ones, we have created the myth of "carefree childhood." How trippingly the phrase falls from the tongue.
Ah, yes.

Ah, hogwash.

But we weave this dream of childhood, this Never-Never Land of barefoot summer days and birthday parties, and assume that all children dwell there blissfully oblivious of the shrapnel of stress which pierces us adults.

Then comes the kicker.

We are jealous of their carefree life, of their getting to romp in this realm of simple pleasures and sustained gratification. School. Vacation. Scouts. Sports. Parties. Later on, full freedom to indulge in all the things we only fantasized.

Damn them.

What a bad rap. But I have seen it, and heard it, and thought it, and felt it. And it is not healthy for anyone.

Even if I were not a father, I would feel better for getting free of that false picture of children's lives.

But I am a father, and my particular children live particular lives at particular ages. As I write, Jad is six. Shannon is ten. Alison is twelve.

The more I can recover how it *really* was to be six, and ten, and twelve, the more I can be available to these three young individuals who share our home and my life. None of them is who I was at their age, but I can stand closer to who they really are at this moment, and be there for them. Being more available, of course, is not an unalloyed blessing.

Having some keener sense of what is happening in a child's life tends to keep me from making decisions petulantly, based on my mood of the moment. I am also aware—sometimes more aware (and feeling more guilty) than I wish—of the children's needs I fail to meet. And I feel more of their pain than I want to— tempting me to shelter them. Besides, I keep supposing there is some potential danger in failing to keep enough psychic distance from my children so that their growing room is not encroached upon. There isn't now any discernible evidence that a problem exists in that area, but it's worth monitoring.

All that notwithstanding, I am grateful to a friend who, ten years ago, gave me a way to feel some of the feelings a child feels, and lured me into a pilgrimage back through the days of my childhood. I found there, in a younger Eliot, a boy who can speak to this father about where his children are.

I grow to like him and them better all the time.

Coursing back through one's childhood memories has its limits, however. To recognize is not necessarily to conquer.

The other anniversary this month—Alison's birthday—made that very clear. It occasioned the reactivation of experiences seared deeply into my own adolescent memory bank.

Judging from the vehemence with which they came to the fore, feelings deposited in memory banks yield a fairly impressive compound interest.

# RIGHT TO BE WRONG
## *or*

## FATHERS ARE NO MORE PERFECTIBLE THAN THEIR CHILDREN

ALISON TURNED TWELVE LAST WEEK.

This week she wants to get her ears pierced.

Over my dead body. That's what I told her. And so she naturally asked me why. She has grown accustomed to asking me why about things. Because, usually, I have a plausible reason or two that she can acknowledge, if not love.

But on this one it's different. I can't give her a reason I'd care to defend in either family debate or forensic. Yet I don't have the luxury of choice. She has been at me for two days now. She has pulled out all the stops, from quiet weeping in despair, to angry crying; from forcefully shouted argument to carefully postured pouting; from one end of the house to the other end of my life:

"What gives you the right to determine whether or not I get my ears pierced?!"

"I've saved my own money for it! It won't cost you a cent!"

"It's not your body! I don't try to tell you what to wear!"

"*All* the kids have them!"

And so on. And on and on and on. Alison is a rather formidable creature under any circumstances, but once aroused and tasting the blood of arbitrariness leaking from an opponent's wounded position, she is awesome.

And she is certainly in no mood to empathize with my hang-up about them. Even though many of my favorite females of all ages wear pierced earrings, I just can't see my own children with them.

It all stems from my own junior high and high school days.

In Fresno, California, no nice girl had pierced ears. That's the way it seemed, anyhow, back in 1950. Only "fast" or poor girls had them. (We used to imagine that all poor girls were fast, but not necessarily vice versa.)

Only three or four girls at our junior high had pierced ears. They also had what it took to enrich one's fantasy life during a boring map study of Eastern Europe, or to stimulate a flood of self-serving lies swapped while waiting for one's "ups" in softball.

"Hey, look, there's ol' Baker. Pretty good stuff."

"Yeah, not bad."

"I've seen better."

"She's real cherry, man."

"How would *you* know, fruit?"

Thus the domino chain of pretending to have carnal knowledge of ol' Baker would abruptly end. When the required affirmation finally came too eagerly and too implausibly from so unlikely a lover as this bespectacled, multi-pimpled waif, the fragile credibility of the whole chain was threatened.

Ol' Baker always had pierced ears.

When we got to high school, the student body included a sprinkling of Mexican kids—and virtually all *those* girls had pierced ears. Almost unfailingly appealing-looking girls, their simple pearl earrings punctuated the soft beige skin of their cheeks and throats.

But we never dated them. They were not our kind—from the other side of the tracks. Their boyfriends were also Mexican, lean and dark; they wore their Levi's very low on their hips, drove '46 Chevy coupes with mudflaps, and smoked a lot.

The boyfriends also had "pachuco" marks on their hands. This homemade tattoo, a cross within a sunburst, was inked between thumb and forefinger, and was the talisman of a community-wide gang of Mexican boys. We Anglos could only imagine what manner of malevolence and mayhem they secretly conspired to commit, under the improper circumstances.

All we knew was that the Mexicans were presumably inferior, and slightly less than human, given their predilection for impaling their ears and inscribing their hands. The only others we'd ever seen do that were on the pages of National Geographic, and were mostly notable for their headdresses, loincloths, and lack of bras.

And now my own daughter wants to join this motley tribe of tramps, trash, and primitives.

Over my dead body.

I know it's irrational. I know ol' Baker wasn't putting out, and the Mexicans weren't inferior, and times have changed. Lots of Alison's friends are lovely young ladies with pierced ears, and she is surely right when she tells me that I would want them if I were she.

And even though there are rational-sounding arguments I could make about her being so young and having lots of time, and about the natural grace of unadorned young womanhood independent of polishes and paints and dyes and earrings, I don't make them.

I just say, this is the way I am, and you'll have to find a way to live with it.

With me, that is.

I MAY BE WRETCHED TO LIVE WITH SOMETIMES BECAUSE of my unrehabilitated history. But the net effect of those thirty-nine years is no worse than what happens to our children by the end of just one long, cold winter. It's now early March, and they have been housebound to an unusual extent this year. We didn't get out much, and I consistently reneged on my promise to take everyone skiing.

Lacking that more favored sport, the children devised another.

I wish they hadn't.

# "STOP YELLING," I SCREAMED

## *or*

### FINDING MYSELF SUCKED INTO THE FRAY AT THEIR LEVEL

IN A NORMAL MATCH PLAY TOURNAMENT, WHETHER GOLF or tennis or whatever, the winners advance to the next round, and the one who wins the most plays the most. Losers are mercifully lopped off, with a minimum of pain. They may play and lose in the first round. Or, they may win a match or two before being knocked off, to sidle away savoring their earlier prosperity.

About the only thing that can prolong a loser's exposure to agony is when a tournament includes the so-called "consolation round" where, presumably, some kinds of people apparently salvage a bit of pride by being the best of the also-rans.

A different kind of tournament erupts in our house from time to time. It gets everyone—and everything—backwards.

It is called teasing.

In teasing everybody loses. A lot.

In this contest, the winner is the one who plays least. The losers have to play on and on, in a sort of disconsolation round that seems interminable, seeking an opponent who can finally lose more than they can.

This is a vicious tournament. It usually starts at the top, and trip-hammers its way down to the youngest. What seems to detonate this chain of fireworks is someone's feeling left out or upstaged. Someone feeling low looks for someone to put down even lower. They inevitably find their prey.

"Too bad you can't go to the pool with us today," a twelve-year-old says with lilting insincerity to a ten-year-old. "But maybe you and the rest of the little kids will find something to play."

"Don't call me a 'little kid.' You know I don't like that!" comes the rejoinder from a not-so-little young lady.

"You don't?" says she, in shocked amazement. "I had no idea. Most little kids don't mind it at all."

"I said, don't call me a little kid!"

"Why, I didn't call you a little kid. I just said that most little kids don't mind being called a . . ."

"Stop it! STOP IT!!" There is shrill menace in her tone.

"Okay, alright," the older girl says in a wounded voice. "Don't be so touchy. Jeesh, all I said was . . ."

The air is split with a shriek. Everybody's in for it now.

I know the fray has started by that particular kind of soaring, wounded howl that arches over my normal threshold of obliviousness to children's wrangling. This piteous cry pierces walls and windows, even shatters my heavy Saturday morning sluggish slumber. I am suddenly bolt upright in bed, wide awake.

More than that. I am fierce with rage. I cannot *stand* to hear one of my children tease another.

They can be *so* cruel. Dominance is established with the first thrust. Then the dominator stands over the victim like a demented surgeon with a rusty scalpel, exploring what vital organs have been laid vulnerable with that quick incision. Poking and probing, tweaking open nerve endings, the dominator evokes a full range of response to the pain, from yelps and howls, to writhing denials of being wounded at all and pathetic counterattacks destined only to increase the strident agony.

Someone's very being is violated and invalidated.

By the time I wake up to what is going on, the original dominator has had her sadistic fill and is curled up, demurely reading a book. But the tournament has barely begun. I come upon the victim-turned-dominator midway into the second round, just as she expertly dodges a wild roundhouse punch her little brother has thrown too blindly in anger, accomplishing only his further humiliation. She is preparing to use the missed punch as further evidence of his utter worthlessness when she sees me coming into the room.

The venom of teasing is so virulent that not even the menacing vision of an enraged father stops her instantly. A last dart is launched and still in mid-air as I scream in savage fury, "Stop it before I smash you all to bits!"

It is not an idle threat.

I really could do it. I feel like hurting them. I haven't, and I won't. But I could. It is a very scary feeling.

Why should teasing turn me into a roaring, grown-up temper tantrum, luring me to the brink of committing mayhem on my own children?

Since I cannot manage to recall many personal child-hood experiences with teasing, the explanation probably lies mainly there, as yet out of reach. One day I will be able to bring it forth, and add it to more accessible explanations.

Like feeling helpless, which prompted my first rage at a child.

It had nothing to do with teasing at all. It was many years ago; the child was still an infant, perhaps a few months old. It was not a Saturday morning, but an anonymous late night. The child was just crying. And crying. And crying.

I was tired and I wanted to go back to bed. I tried everything, but nothing worked. Not the bottle. Nor the pacifier. Nor burping, cooing, singing, threatening.

I was helpless. My efforts meant nothing. I became enraged.

Then I felt like dashing the child against the wall, to bring peace to both of us.

But I didn't. And I wouldn't.

The thought electrified me. I really could have devastated that child.

All at once I knew that child-beaters were not wholly other than I. They were not inexplicably despicable monsters. We were part of one another, distinct only for something's having triggered a restraint in me, just a millisecond this side of our being indistinguishable.

I am struck by the common factor of my being helpless, both at a crying baby's cribside and amidst a gory teasing bout.

I lack the power to impose control on the uncontrolled impulses of a child. Nor am I able to stimulate their self-control.

So I lose my own.

Doesn't make any sense, except as a description of what really happens. I guess I have difficulty letting some things happen, even though they are bound to. Babies will cry. Children will tease.

But I am *not* bound to blow up, if I can get some distance from feeling that I should be able to control the situation. Maybe because I know how mean and volcanic personal feelings can be, I should concentrate on helping the children to achieve self-control during less hostile times, and then hope it tempers their abuse of each other when the inevitable savagery breaks out.

More important, though, may be the ongoing effort to help them feel good about themselves. I think that cuts two ways. It may strengthen the self-control, but it also could dampen their vulnerability to feeling attacked at the core of their worth. It does seem to be the very self which is demeaned during a teaser's onslaught, and it must be the defense of that self which elicits the furious response and impels the subsequent selection of an opponent against whom that worth can be finally proved and restored.

If children's right to be who they are would not always be up for grabs, it might be a little easier for them to keep a cool head. Maybe that was the point of all those times I wishfully insisted, to myself or others, that sticks and stones might break my bones but names would never hurt me.

Never hurt me, or change me, or invalidate me.

That was good to know, as a child. No wonder that shibboleth is transmitted from one generation of children to the next.

Now, if I can just get in touch with those times it *didn't* work for me . . .

THE END OF OUR WINTER-LONG CABIN FEVER IS IN SIGHT.
March did its duty, after having come in like a lion. It went out like a lamb, and so did my little lambs, out into the sunshine and warmth to exorcise some pretty wintry spirits.

My lambs did not go out to cavort, however, on their own two hooves. They wanted their bicycles to ride. So we needed our annual day-long "bicycle clinic" during which I strive both to cure whatever ailments have beset the bikes since the fall and to teach the children how to do it themselves next time.

Neither facet of the clinic was a rousing success.

Both the bikes and the children are a little more complicated than I remember from my youth.

# THE CURSE OF AFFLUENCE
## or

*I THOUGHT THESE GADGETS WOULD SERVE ME WELL. WHAT THEY REALLY DO IS SERVE ME RIGHT.*

"WHY DON'T WE HAVE A LITTLE BIKE HIKE THIS WEEK-end," suggests Patti one night at dinner. "It'd be good for us all to get out of the house."

Shannon seconds the idea with a word: "Neat!"

"We could go Saturday morning—it'd do us good to get away from that stupid TV anyhow—" Patti continues, "and ride out to Herrontown Woods for our first stop."

"In the *morning*?" counters Alison. "It's the only morning of the week when Jennifer and I can get together. The afternoons are all . . ."

"Yeah," chimes in Jad. "And since I only get to watch two TV shows the whole rest of the week that's the only time . . ."

"You can get along without them for one Saturday," I observe helpfully.

"What I had in mind," Patti continues, "was fixing us a picnic breakfast. We could have some hardboiled eggs and English muffins, a thermos of hot chocolate and some orange juice. I'll wrap the eggs and muffins so they'll still be warm when we get there. C'mon, you guys, it would really be fun."

"I think it sounds neat!" enthuses Shannon, and Alison and Jad concur.

"But," Alison remembers, "my bike is all wrecked up."

"What do you mean," I ask, "by 'all wrecked up'? Exactly what is wrong with it?"

"You remember, Dad, last fall, when the gears jammed and I couldn't ride to the fellowship picnic at Marquand Park? We never got it fixed."

Swell.

From my left, Shannon asks, "Did you ever replace the cable on my hand brakes? 'Cause if you didn't, they need fixing too."

"That's just great," I mutter. "And how about you, Jad? I suppose we need to rebuild your bike, too."

"Nope," he chirps.

"Well, thank heavens for small favors—"

"No problems with my bike," he reiterates, "because somebody ripped it off, remember? I just need a new one."

I also remember that I have not filed the insurance claims so we can recover some portion of the small fortune a bike costs these days.

Imagine.

In the course of just five minutes, we have gone from a tentative proposal for a morning's family idyll, through reluctance, up to high enthusiasm on the part of all, clear back down to the pits of despondency—on my part—as I see a mountain of mechanical junk standing between me and a picnic breakfast in Herrontown Woods with Patti and the kids.

By this time I feel like I've been marinated in vinegar and could not care less whether we go on the bike hike.

Where did I go wrong?

I have done what I thought I was supposed to do. When I grew up, I found work that would pay me enough to buy my kids all those mechanical toys that I yearned to have but couldn't afford as a child. And I fetched some goodies for my wife, and for myself. Top-of-the-line equipment, too. Not simple stuff like we used to have when I was a kid.

My first bike was secondhand. I didn't get it until I was ten, when I bought it from a guy on my newspaper route who'd had it in his garage for years. A faded blue beauty, with about a hundred pound frame, and fenders five or six inches wide arching over some chainlink-tread tires riddled with cracks along the sidewalls.

It took me about three days to get enough Neverleak into the tires to pack them full, and probably didn't cost me much more than a pair of new tires and tubes would have. But once I got it rolling, that bike never let me down. It was disabled only once—when my best friend and I became curious about how a coaster brake was put together. We got only as far as finding out how one comes apart.

My kids, though—they've got ten-speed gearshifts and handbrakes. And racing tires. And lightweight frames. And trouble.

I do the best I can to fix anything that resembles the parts bikes had when I was a kid. But, increasingly, I am in over my head and have to turn to some high-priced pro to fix them up.

The bikes are in the bike shop, maybe every other month. Times three kids. Broken cables and spring tune-ups and transmission overhauls, everything but pollution control devices to go wrong. Ten bucks here, thirty bucks there. Perhaps over the long haul I'd make out better if I fixed everything myself, but it's the initial investment that slows me down—tools, machine shop, parts inventory, two weeks of factory training. Not to mention spending half of the rest of my life grudgingly applying my new talents.

It's just as bad with our cars. I'd always dreamed of having one of these big boats with power antenna and signal-seeking stereo radio and hide-away headlights and electric windows and thermostatically controlled air conditioning and leather seats.

I got one. So far, only the leather seats have not given me any trouble.

At midnight, at five above zero, in an airport parking lot, at the end of a long and exhausting overseas business trip, when I wanted nothing more than to be at home snuggling in a warm bed with my wife, Patti, the headlight eyelids froze closed. It was a long time before I got home to my wife, and I minded it. A lot.

Think not that the car takes more kindly to hot weather, though. With both the temperature and the humidity in the nineties, the vacuum system which controls the air conditioning vents, which are activated by the thermostat, which also regulates the compressor's cold air output, went kaput. No air output.

I was enroute to a Very Important meeting, the kind on which one's career appears to hang. And if, in reliance on the air conditioning, my car had not been laden with seven hundred pages of unbound proposals, carefully arranged in seven stacks for binding immediately upon arrival at the Very Important meeting, I might have electrically lowered my windows for a bit of breeze.

Doggedly loping along the broiling turnpike, I blinked away the drops of sweat trickling down from my brow, while my tortured mind taunted me with visions of the blue 1936 Ford sedan which for years made its reliable way through several generations of my family.

It was air conditioned. There was this nice, smooth, brown cast-metal fan about the size of your fist, mounted on the dashboard. At the solid click of a simple on-off toggle switch, three petal-like rubber blades whirled and wafted the breeze wherever you pointed them. Then you popped open the cowl vent, to cool your feet. If that weren't enough, when you were really rolling you shoved the vent windows open, to chisel off twin torrents of air that converged somewhere around your lap. Now there was real air conditioning.

By the time that car got to me, the rubber fan blades were granulating and the edges of the vent windows looked like someone had caulked them with coddled egg whites. But you never wasted any of your life trying to *fix* it.

Cold weather never bothered that car's headlights, either. They sat right out there like lovely steel and glass melons, where you could see and feel all around them—and where they could see out.

Now you just have to trust me, that what I tell you next is true: as I am sitting here at my typewriter, writing this chapter, right here—this page—the phone rings. It is Patti calling. It is about the car. The car sits wheezing in front of the children's music school, spewing a mystery fluid all over the road. So help me God.

I like to write. Outside of sailing or making love or good conversation over a couple of drinks with interesting people, there's nothing I'd rather do. But now I've got to interrupt this sublime pleasure to mind the needs of our mechanical marvel. I will, however, be back with some heartfelt words about this kind of goings-on.

I am back—and somewhat pushed out of shape. All these damned machines and gadgets, all the things I bought thinking they would serve me well; they suck the life right out of me, an hour at a time. Traipsing back and forth to repair shops, I see precious chunks of life being paid out as ransom for my addiction to consumer goods.

I have to learn to kick the habit; the price is too high. Every purchase I make, and the inevitable time it will eventually cost in care and feeding, serves mainly to divert me from the genuine joys of living—being with my family and other friends, writing, sailing, building, daydreaming. I don't blame anybody else. It's not the fault of the manufacturers of the products, or the fault of the manufacturer of the dreams. I am the one who let myself invest significance in the goods, and now I am paying a dearer price than ever I could have imagined.

Quitting smoking was a trifle compared with weaning myself away from all this junk. I am drawn to a smaller, simpler automobile, for instance, but I'd love to sneak in just an electric window or two, to still show that I've made it. I cannot go all the way to the Volkswagen Beetle.

It's even harder with the kids. How can I not buy them three-speed or five-speed or ten-speed bikes when every other kid on the block has one? By today's standards, my old bike was no dream, but neither were my friends' bikes. Not many of them bought the super Schwinns with tank horns and spring suspension front forks being ridden across slick brochures by Bing Crosby and his family at Pebble Beach. But the trouble now is that it's difficult to impose an austerity or simplicity kick on my children, because I think that they would feel out of it and dumb.

I don't know what to do. Struggle, I guess, and try to keep remembering what really matters in my life. Try to remember that all this junk we buy gets in the way of being with people.

People matter.

But being close to people is also pretty demanding, and sometimes painful. Maybe we preoccupy ourselves with selecting and buying (and fixing) all this stuff we own as a diversion—from each other. Maybe we buffer ourselves from each other's needs by fixing our gaze on goods.

That is not a model I want to set, if I can help it.

But it sure is hard to live by what you *believe,* when everything around you says to live by what you see.

THAT QUANDARY—WHETHER TO LIVE BY INNER VALUES
and intimate relationships, or by outer trappings and
public approbation—has been felt more keenly by recent
generations of students than by the rest of us, I think.
I used to work closely with high school students, in the
mid- and late sixties, as a young minister organizing
youth groups and social action projects. Those kids
struggled hard with significant questions.

I have tried, over the ensuing years, to keep in touch
with some of these pilgrims to see how they are making
out (and to keep me open to asking the right questions).

For years, I could expect lots of visitors about this
time of year as colleges let out for spring break and
the kids came to call. But now that generation has
grown up, dispersed, and—as a culture—dissolved. Most
of its members are part of the mainstream. A couple
of them are even professional colleagues of mine.

So I don't expect those springtime harbingers of an
ascendant alternate life style to appear at my door as
they used to. But I do get an occasional surprise. Like
last night.

He hadn't changed at all. There isn't anything sad-
der I could say.

For almost eight full years, from age sixteen to age
twenty-four, he must have hidden out in a kind of
suspended animation, somehow fearing to kindle the
spirit of his own being.

Four years of undergraduate work, from which only the most desultory residue could be elicited. Another four years of graduate work, with no discernible benefit. More "study" lay ahead, he supposed.

He reminded me of those vagrant snowflakes that sometimes blow down on a gray and chilly spring day —too puny to make a storm, too late to be part of winter, too dispirited to take part in spring.

And then I remembered how difficult it was for kids in the sixties to discern what anyone really *believed*. The world was so full of fears and phonies and lies and raw impulses. Belief in anything, in any*one*, seemed too much to ask.

Many parents and children had difficulty believing in each other. Some, like my stunted guest, never recovered. When he left, I remembered what I had learned back then.

# IT AIN'T HOW YOU DO IT
## *or*

## *LEARNING TO BE SATISFIED WITH LIKING YOUR CHILDREN*

1969.

Sunday night, late. A fire burning. Good Scotch in my glass. I sank into my favorite chair wanting not to think, and mindlessness came easily. The weekend's work had left me sodden, spent of every spark of imagination and energy.

Starting early Saturday morning, they had come at hourly intervals—on through the day until early evening, then starting again Sunday right after worship until late, until now, when I found it so effortless to let them all become a blur. Teenagers, for the most part, and their parents. All coming to this minister who worked with "youth," wanting to know what was wrong with them or with each other.

I had listened carefully—empathically, I thought— and struggled to find among my inadequate clinical tools some technique to make a corrective twist to their very usual problems. And now I was tired.

But more so than usual, because as of that weekend it seemed to me that I had seen every conceivable style of child-rearing represented by unhappy children and unhappy parents. No, more than miserable—really screwed up. And so we sat there before the fire, Patti and I, as I struggled to retrieve some particular faces and families from the gloomy army that had paraded through that weekend. Who were they? What were they like? What did they have in common?

If the way in which they raised their children seemingly made little difference in their happiness, what did?

The questions helped us focus, and the faces of real people re-emerged from the weekend's amorphous bulk. Early Saturday, the seventeen-year-old girl who was secretly engaged had told me of her evening the night before, and the dream which had followed. She had been home watching TV with her parents. But she was yearning to be out with the young man for whom she was knitting a sweater before the TV.

But they had plans for her education, and her getting married did not fit into their arrangements for her. The merits for the principals of such a marriage had never been discussed, so far as I knew. But there seemed some conventional wisdom to the parents' position—"not till you've finished college"—that appealed to a middle-class sense of educational symmetry, and I found myself instinctively somewhat on their "side."

She had told me her dream. That night she saw herself as an old woman of seventy, sitting in that same chair. Standing over her was her mother, now in her nineties, knitting her into a straitjacket that enveloped the chair: a permanent cocoon to rot away in, without ever knowing metamorphosis.

We had talked about it, and she was surprised to recognize that she was making no effort to resist this mummification. She began to understand the symbiotic nature of the problem with her parents, and her very passive complicity in it.

But it didn't help me with my problem. Her parents were unexceptional to a fault—orderly, charitable, soft-spoken—who seemed to treat both their daughter and her brother with respect. They had high hopes for their children, as we all do, and I couldn't see anything they were doing wrong.

Nor could I find much to disdain in the style of the parents of an intermittently suicidal fourteen-year-old. They were strict and strait-laced, but they weren't repressive. Nor in the laissez-faire approach of a pair of very respected Ph.D. parents whose sixteen-year-old son had flunked out of all his classes as his abuse of drugs had made Swiss cheese of his once-fine mind.

And so the review went fruitlessly on, making allowances for the obvious pathologies of alcoholic parents, and savage post-divorce battles with children as pawns, and power-addicted fathers who insisted on their sons' scoring big, as they had.

The confounding part was that, for every instance of parenting style which involved a screwed-up kid, I could think of a really healthy counterpart who had not only survived the parenting style but somehow thrived under it. I mined my memory, back past the weekend's traffic to other teenagers I had known well in previous jobs— students in a small New England coed college, students in a California high school—and the contradiction held true. Strict or soft, ad hoc or riddled with rules, different parenting styles seemed to be equally capable of producing children who were sound and children who were unsteady.

Was there *any* common denominator? If not among the parents of the troubled kids, then how about among the parents of the hundreds who kept moving ahead?

Yes. Suddenly it was right there: *They really dig their kids.*

Those were the words that came, clear and indelible.

It is not an elegant phrase, and I have tried in the years since to re-articulate it, to give it a bit more class and polish and precision. But it doesn't want to be messed around with: They really dig their kids.

Surely there must be a finer way to put it. And "dig," after all, is such a passé term. How about "like" or "admire" or "love"?

They're all part of it, but "dig" goes deeper. It means the parents are glad those children are *their* children. The parents delight in them, when they're not screaming at them. (Or, in spite of the fact that they sometimes scream at them.) The parents occasionally marvel at them, continuingly refreshed by the wonder of what those children invent and create and think and feel and say.

The kids who come up healthy don't seem to have any fewer hassles with their parents. They, too, think their parents anywhere from simply corny to authentically outrageous about this or that. They chafe at limits, if their parents are limit-setters; or they yearn for limits, if their parents don't set them. They want more or less help than they get in choosing friends and movies and schools and clothes.

But they have gotten the message, and for the most

part never doubt for a minute that they are just about the best thing that ever happened to their mother and father.

Parents who dig their kids seem to know that they owe a lot of their own humanity to their children.

That's the hooker, of course. You have to like who you are before you can be glad about the people who got you that way.

SOMETIMES I THINK I'D LIKE MYSELF A BIT BETTER IF I were a little more methodical. I have occasion to contemplate that possibility annually, just about this time.

April 15.

My financial records are in a hopeless state of disarray. I never keep receipts. I never balance my checkbook. I never know whether or to whom I have paid anything, from property taxes to children's allowances.

As for the allowances, at least, there are *three* someones to monitor my performance and let me know where I stand.

In more ways than one.

# HE WHO PAYS THE PIPER
# (Ought to Find Out
# What the Piper Likes to Play)

ALLOWANCES COME DUE ON THE FIRST OF THE MONTH.

Jad makes sure I remember that. He has had, after all, somewhere in the neighborhood of twenty-nine or thirty days of pennilessness during which he could contemplate the glacially slow approach of the magic day.

Jad, aged six, blows his money.

Even as he stands there, hand out, feet shuffling in an anxious little dance step, he is rattling off some pseudo-Globetrotter jive talk about where his allowance is going.

"Slap it to me, Daddy-O. Got some big buying to do today."

"Where you headed, pal?"

"Down to the hobby shop, to dig me a model."

"Got anything particular in mind?" I ask, knowing full well he does.

"You better believe it, man!" Then, he suddenly

shifts gears from groovy hipster to earnest seeker of truth: "Dad," he says, as the body tension subsides, "which do you think is a better deal—a plastic model of a stunt plane, to go with my other planes, or a wooden model?"

"You haven't done a wooden model yet, have you?"

"No. And that's just it. I'd like to try one, but I don't want to mess it up. Otherwise, my whole allowance is gone, for nothing, and that really makes me angry."

He is speaking from experience.

We talk a bit about the pros and cons of each option. He finally decides he's not ready to tackle the wooden model. Too time-consuming for the rewards involved.

Now his wiry body is overcome once again with St. Vitus's dance and the Globetrotter badinage is rhythmically restored: "Two-place stunt plane, here I come. Can you dig it?" he yelps, relieved and energized.

With the purification of his sugarplum vision, he is suddenly possessed of kinetic furies which will propel him hopping and skipping the few blocks to the hobby shop. Once there, he will rid himself of every last cent only minutes after I almost ruefully lay the cash in his hand.

But for once, I let *him* decide how to spend it.

And I've nearly accepted how suddenly, how totally it's all over. All gone. Nothing left for a long month to come.

Used to be, I messed around a lot in how and when the children spent their money. It just drove me bananas to see them dump their meager treasury on the variety-store counter and stride out caressing some abysmally ill-formed, cynically overpriced, unforgivably garish little plaster creature destined to chip today, break tomorrow, and be abandoned by sunup of the third day.

So I gave them lots of advice—sensible, sound, informative, and, beyond all doubt, helpful.

"Don't you think *this* would be nice, honey? Built to last a lifetime, and it just matches the drapery hardware in your bedroom."

And so, one by one, I would spend their allowances for them, coyly suckering them into buying the kind of things any adult in his late thirties would just love if he felt responsible for scrutinizing and supervising the expenditure of two dollars . . .

On the way home, I usually felt constrained to do a little artificial respiration, puffing a few breaths of paternalistic enthusiasm for the sensible purchase, hoping to inflate the row of shoulders which sagged just a trace across the back seat.

Then one day Alison's sag slid into a skulk, pouty enough to demand my attention.

"You look unhappy."

"Wouldn't *you* be?"

"Wouldn't I be, if what?"

"If you had somebody telling you how to spend your allowance!"

"Yeah," Shannon chimed in. "You don't think kids are smart enough to spend their own money without the advice of a grown-up." The word "grown-up" had the scent of wine vinegar about it.

Alison muttered, "Can't ever get what you want without feeling guilty . . ."

"But I was just trying to help, to . . . to keep you . . ."

Shannon interrupted, suddenly vibrant with feeling:

"To keep us from making a mistake, I bet."

"Yes. Exactly. And what's wrong with that?" I asked, and knew the answer even as I spoke.

Jad will be home any minute now. I don't know yet the particular plane he bought, but I do know what brand it is. He has made a lot of purchases in the last two years. Unaided. And some of them were mistakes. He knows which ones. Without my telling him. And now he knows which brand is best.

When he first got interested in models, I liked to make them for him. I mean, with him. Now he just asks me for help when he has a particularly difficult assembly problem—usually one which takes more than two hands. And I'm content to consult and construct by invitation only. I like to see what happens when the children make their own decisions.

Being invited to "butt out" has rewards, after it stops smarting. Every time I find a new way to let go, they find a new way to grow. Better for them, better for me.

They need the freedom to become who they are, and I need the time to work on the wooden sailboat model Patti thoughtfully gave me to absorb my surplus interest in such things.

PATTI AND I ARE QUITE DIFFERENT CREATURES. WHEN there's a conflict, it is she who thinks through an appealing alternative to bloodshed, or territorial encroachment. She is equally good at constructive diversion, when that is the wiser course for a child.

Or an adult.

She is also fairer and tougher than I am, willing to bear the day-in-and-day-out jostling that befalls fulltime arbitrators. I am more likely to cut and run, especially now that fair weather lures me to the tennis court. I feel guilty, of course, about being out having fun playing tennis while Patti is doing the real scut work of parenting.

So I slink home behind a fanfare of jollity. I exude enthusiasm for having played and having played well. At such moments I am very malleable.

I am beginning to suspect my children notice.

And take advantage.

# DIFFERENT STROKES FOR DIFFERENT FOLKS

*or*

*WATCHING HOW A CHILD EVOKES THE NEEDED PARENTING*

WHEN I DID SOMETHING WRONG AS A CHILD, I JUST HOPED my parents wouldn't find out. Never mind that they usually did. My way of dealing with the heavy knowledge of my wrongdoing was to pretend it didn't exist.

I spent a lot of time worrying, those days. Worrying that Mrs. Sabatino would call to tell them about the rock I had put through the front window of their shoe repair shop. Or that Mr. Rattray would call about the stone through his garage window. Or that Mr. Talbot would call about the rows of windows in his garage, shot out with a BB gun.

Actually, I didn't worry quite so much about Mr. Talbot, because another kid and I did it together, with the other kid's gun. His name was Tommy Talbot.

But Mrs. Sabatino did call.

"He was throwing a rock at my son, Carl, your son," she would say, "and it missed poor Carl, praise the Lord. No thanks to your boy, I might say. So it hit the shop window, the rock. It'll be forty dollars."

My mother was the one who usually got these calls and was unfailingly courteous on the phone. She knew all her lines, having had a fair amount of practice with four such sons.

I can't remember what happened when she hung up.

Now I have two daughters and a son, and sometimes they do something wrong. And, no doubt, worry about it.

One has unwittingly adopted their father's ostrich stance, head in the sands of pretended ignorance and tail teed up for the inevitable. The other two each have a different, personal style.

One compulsively returns to the scene of the crime with parent in tow. I'm not always quick to grasp the significance of being led, say, into the workshop by this suddenly semi-mute, quirky-acting kid. But a look around the room usually turns up the impulsion for our mission—an overturned gallon of paint, perhaps. Opened, needless to say, without permission,

The remaining child favors sinking blackly into a too-obvious moping, sodden with dismal grief. A more pathetic picture of utterly hopeless humanity never piqued your curiosity.

"I have the feeling something's bothering you," I invite.

Mournful nod of assent, eyes anchored heavily to the floor.

"Maybe you'd like to tell me about it."

Whatever "it" is, is obviously too terrible to be spoken—not, at least, for another minute or two, while a full range of tragic fantasies plays through my mind. Such is the intended backdrop, I eventually came to realize, against which the eventual revelation of wrong-doing would appear so inconsequential as to merit little follow-through.

"Oh," I am supposed to exclaim with relief, "your failure to put your dog in his kennel *didn't* lead to his peeing all over the white carpet in the living room, chewing up the new sofa, and eating the roast that was thawing for company dinner tonight?"

Lighter nod of assent.

"He just peed all over the carpet."

"Uh-huh."

That is supposed to sound like good news.

Now, this range of techniques is employed when managing a peccadillo vis-à-vis their *father*. Each has a variation on the theme if Patti is the probable recipient of the news.

But that's another story. And not the point I think I'm coming to. Which is, even though I know I am being "handled," I respond pretty predictably to each child's approach. Predictably, and differently, as the different children call the tune.

Somewhere along the line, I became troubled by my differing reactions to the children's getting in trouble. One I yelled at, another I disciplined constructively, a third I wound up comforting, of all things.

And I felt guilty about the disparity, guilty about blowing up at only one of them, guilty about my capriciousness and inconsistency. Did I play favorites? Was I lacking standards? What was going on?

Then it came to me: They're asking for it.

*They* are the ones who set the terms by which such conflicts are managed. They set me up to react the way

I do. If they wanted me to react differently toward them, they'd adopt the oft-observed methods of their siblings.

But each must have found the most satisfying way for them, personally, to have me respond.

They call the tune, and somehow seem to get what they need—even if it isn't always what they would *want*, given a chance to undo the wrongdoing.

Which leads me to wonder if it wouldn't make some sense to establish the use of "child" as a verb. As in, "There are a variety of ways to child one's parents."

Just like there are a variety of ways to parent one's children.

Each childs me differently, when guilty. One seems to need the thunderclap of indignation when father has heard, from a third party, what's been going on. Another prefers mild congratulations for having led me to the mess—and a partnership in setting it right. The third apparently needs some propping up, because the burden of having fallen is too weighty to manage alone.

And so each "childs" me in a way designed to evoke from me the kind of parenting they need.

I think that may happen a lot—lots more than I recognize or suspect. Even though I am one man, with a relatively limited range of responses, these three play me in highly personal styles, like so many musicians at an instrument. They evoke from me responsive notes that harmonize with, and make chords of, the discord they feel.

They play on Patti just as skillfully. But their technique at such times is very different; it is much more passive, so that she has to supply most of the energy for the dialogue.

A woefully overdue library book turns up.

"Who checked out *Pinch a Dream?*"

Three blank faces in the lineup. Not a trace of emotion or recognition in any of them.

"Well?"

"Not me," says Jad, adding with a toss of his head, "that's one of those dumb love stories. Probably Alison."

"It *is not* mine. Don't go accusing people when you don't know what you're talking about, pea-brain."

"Don't call me . . ."

"STOP! We're not here to squabble. I just want to know who checked this book out, because *some*body owes fifty-two cents in overdue fines."

Silence.

That's the way they child her, with silence. Because they know what will come next.

"Swell. Am I supposed to pay it myself, because none of my children will own up to their responsibility?"

"Wellll . . ." ventures Shannon with a mixture of relief and annoyance, "I'll pay it—but not because it's mine."

And thus the matter is resolved.

Sort of.

Because Patti still doesn't have a sure sense of who really checked out *Pinch a Dream* in the first place. For Shannon is perfectly capable of bearing the sins of others, just to spare her mother the injustice of it all.

And Alison and Jad are perfectly capable of letting her. Sort of like their father.

Shannon has, in Patti, a good model of someone who cares a lot—so much, in fact, that some object lessons get short-circuited.

"Who is responsible for feeding the rabbit this week?"

Again, three blank faces in the lineup. Not a trace of emotion or recognition in any of them.

"Well?"

"Not me," says Jad. "Probably Alison."

"I am *not*, jer—"

"STOP! We're not going to get into hassles with each other. Meantime the poor rabbit is starving. All I care about is finding out who is responsible for feeding the rabbit, so he can get fed."

"Well," begins Alison, "I'm *supposed* to have it this week, but Shannon left everything in such a mess from last week that . . ."

"What do you mean?!" Patti demands.

"What do you mean?" Shannon asks, limply defensive.

"Never mind that, Shannon," Patti orders. "Are you telling me that the poor rabbit has not been fed since *last week?!*"

Silence.

"Well?"

"The reason it was a mess," Shannon begins with a rush, "is that I had to tear up the whole stupid place looking for the new bag of pellets."

"They were in the back end of the station wagon," Patti says matter-of-factly. Then a trace of alarm comes into her voice. "You *did* find them there, didn't you?"

"Ohhhh, so *that's* where they were!"

Patti is apoplectic. "Don't tell me . . . No, don't tell me that poor rabbit hasn't had any . . . *Two* weeks?! No. I just can't believe it." She slumps, sick at heart.

Silence.

Then she begins, deliberately, in a controlled rage. "That rabbit is our pet. He cannot go out and forage for himself. The reason he can't is because we made a kind of promise to him, to take care of him in return for his staying locked in our cage."

She pauses for effect. A few muted flickers of emotion

play around the children. Are they uncomfortable because of the plight of the rabbit, their own culpability, or their mother's performance?

"Without food and water, fresh *every single day,* he will die. We will have killed him. We will have *murdered* him."

Pause.

Silence.

"*Some*body has to go take care of that rabbit. Immediately." The burden thus laid on their hearts, she leaves the room heavily. Or however a 101-pounder manages to convey the feeling.

The children look at each other uneasily, exchange a few parting shots over whose fault it was in the first place, and go about their business—secure in the knowledge that Patti has succeeded in making the case so piteously that within moments the rabbit will be fed, watered, cuddled, and apologized to.

By Patti herself.

But our children child us in good times, too. When the report card brings a smile; as well as when blemishes dot it. When some art work wins a contest, as well as when unauthorized graffiti appear on a driveway. When the dog responds to training, as well as when . . .

And if I am careful to listen for what they want to evoke from me as counterpart to their interior state, something comes over me. A heightened sense of their uniqueness; that they *are* unique, brand-new creatures under the sun, not like any others who ever were. Making their way among us, with us, through us. Becoming.

Very becoming.

SPRINGTIME IN PRINCETON.

Long before we moved here, friends had told us of its glory. And every spring the promise is fulfilled beyond measure.

Whenever Patti and I are in the car, we detour through country lanes in the farmland surrounding our town, just to revel in the expanse of nature's becoming.

This spring our revelry took on an added dimension.

# THE GRASS IS ALWAYS GREENER

## *or*

## *SOME DREAMS ARE BETTER SLEPT ON THAN LIVED WITH*

PATTI AND I HAD DRIVEN PAST THAT OLD FARM A HUNDRED times. It stands right on the fringe of town, marking the boundary between houses-on-lots and country places.

The stately white house is ringed with a pillared old porch, surveying the broad lawns which sweep out in every direction under the ancient trees arching over all. The barn and outbuildings are nestled discreetly under some particularly dense trees at the edge of the woods. Hedges and stonework and gravel drives describe patterns of order across the property.

We had driven past the place a hundred times. And a hundred times one had said to the other, "Wouldn't it be . . ."

Now we crested the hill and there was the sign: For Sale. Just like that. After three generations in the same family, it was up for grabs.

Good thing the children weren't with us. Trying to discipline their fantasies would not only have been impossible, but would also have hampered our letting our own dreams run riot. It was *our* turn to be childlike, chattering wildly about where we would build the corral for the horses we'd surely have, about finding a big old-fashioned porch swing on which we could slip away balmy evenings, about making echoes of the olden days on that farm come alive and lively again.

Within the hour a realtor was showing us through the cool and empty expanse of the old house. We heard scarcely a word she spoke, preoccupied with touching finely turned woodwork and hardware, plotting who would sleep where, fancying gala parties of admiring friends warming the main rooms.

And won't it be fabulous for the children, we told each other. All the benefits of farm life, yet within an easy bike ride of town. They will have horses, of course, and all manner of four- and two-legged companions. Think of the happy hours in the barn on a rainy day! Imagine the industrious projects abuilding in the cavernous drive-in basement! Oh, and the space to ramble through endless halls and attics and stairways! Truly, it will be the greatest thing that ever happened to them.

Yes, I told the real estate lady, we're very, very interested. Both Patti and I have to dash off to previous appointments, but we'll be in touch later today. Stay near your phone.

We drove out the winding drive gently, stopping several times before we got to the road, savoring the spell of magic about the old place. Oh, the children will love it! Lucky kids!

We were still a block away from our home when the mournful barking of Alison's dog seeped into the car. We tracked it to its source—the backyard pen where he had been left, without water, all day.

Again.

The scene—helpless barking and the barren water dish—burned like acid through the gossamer fantasy of *our* children resourcefully running a mini-farm. The euphoric cloud sagged. That is simply not who they are and we know it.

Admirable qualities they possess in abundance, to be sure. But faithful tending of chores is least among them.

And no honor would be done our children, or our family life, if we were to install ourselves on that farm with the facile assumption that we did so because it would be great for the kids. They could not be counted on to become reliable little farmhands, and shouldn't be, and we knew it.

No, if we were going to pull the dream of that farm into reality, we must find a better reason.

We were not without alternatives.

Everything about the farm evoked personal dreams of long standing. Patti had loved horses all her life, and she had had one once. But it had come a little too late. Her parents managed finally to afford it just when a teenage girl begins to think more about other teenagers than about private pursuits. And so her early equestrienne days were bittersweet, compromising her time for joining the gang in newer pleasures, leaving her ambivalent and, eventually, unfulfilled.

The farm was a second chance for her time as a horsewoman.

It was a second chance for me, too. Not that I had ever really loved horses. Rather, I had loved the idea of horses. After all, that's what all the successful people had. Stallions and mares prancing through the free-floating images of success: priceless race horses in spotless stables, set amid lush pastures; virile polo ponies awaiting the command of sleek playboys at a sumptuous tailgate picnic; trusted Shetlands drawing the manorborn across the grounds in pony carts of wicker and brass and lacquer and leather.

A squire, at last.

Yes, we're very interested, I told the real estate lady. Please meet us at the farm at once.

As we drove there, Patti and I congratulated ourselves. We had avoided saddling our children with an inappropriate network of expectations. Now, at least, we knew who we were buying the place for, and why.

Cresting the hill, we came gladly under the spell all over again. God willing, endless generations of Daleys would henceforth reign here—our rightful homestead, now and forever.

We strode the house and grounds with new vision.

Yes, Patti, you can have the horses, and it matters not whether the children indenture themselves to our ambitions. And I will make the basement redolent with fresh wood shavings, a veritable Santa's workshop. Perchance the little tykes will apprentice themselves from time to time, but no matter if they don't.

And together we shall grandly receive our envious guests who days afterward will no doubt marvel at my material success.

Funny, it was the real estate agent and her boss who unwittingly blew the whistle on our dreams of grandeur.

We had asked her to come home with us and evaluate our house for a quick sale. After five years of extensive remodeling to make the place just right for the way we live, we had only a vague idea what it might fetch on the market.

She walked in the door, looked around, and asked

why we would ever want to leave such a nice house in such a nice location.

I pretended not to hear.

Then she said it was worth 50 percent more than I would have supposed. I was astonished. Perhaps, I suggested tactfully, it would be reassuring to get a corroborating estimate.

When her boss arrived a few minutes later, he looked around and asked why we would want to leave such a nice home in such a nice location. And yes, by the way, it's worth half again as much as you thought.

Of course the market value of our home made the farm all the more feasible financially, and the flurry of excited exchanges between Patti and me continued for several hours after the realtors left.

But the real question lasted just a bit longer.

It was still there, patient and persistent, late that night. Why *would* we want to leave the way we live? All the hours we would pour into that farm—what would they displace? What would we relinquish while claiming postponed dreams? Time with each other? Evenings with friends? Trips or games or just horsing around with our children? Commitments to church, or professions, or important causes?

Singly, and together, we drove past the farm a half dozen times during the next couple of days. The passion was still there, at first. Then wistfulness crept in to quell it. A touch of resoluteness surged up, just to keep some order. And finally, almost no feeling at all.

But quite a bit of feeling about our life. Like it's worth half again as much as we thought.

Maybe more.

WE MAY NOT HAVE A FARM, AND OUR CHILDREN MAY not be farmhands at heart, but that doesn't keep us from harboring an interior barnyard full of animals. That none of them has died of neglect is a tribute to Patti, and not to anyone else.

Although she would gladly share the honors.

But there are no takers.

I myself am not for *letting* them die, you understand. However, if they just happen to complete their pre-ordained life cycle, well, eventually we can reclaim whole portions of the house for human beings.

When the roll is called up yonder for felines, I have a nomination.

# SIBLING FIDELITY

## *or*

### TAPPING THE RESERVOIR OF INEXPRESSIBLE CARE FOR EACH OTHER

WE HAVE A CAT.

Actually, that's not strictly true. What I mean to say is, Alison has a cat. "Gypsy" is the sole survivor of a trio of cats once owned by my trio of children.

I do not like cats. At all. No cat I have ever known has given me any direct cause to justify its continued sustenance at my expense.

I will concede that there are indirect causes. Namely, my children love them. And I love my children and try, within limits, to satisfy their desires.

But my personal experience of cats has been less than satisfactory. Cats climb up my body. Whether drawn by my particular contour or fragrance or what, I do not know. You'd have to ask them. One minute a cat is slowly winding itself around my ankle, like a magician wrapping a silken scarf around his hand, and the next minute—ascent!

Cats do not climb well unless their claws are well

extended, and find purchase in some substantial turf, like flesh.

Mine.

I have a well-defined reaction to this experience. It is called pain. And I don't like it much. Therefore, I give other people's cats a wide berth, and give Gypsy no berth at all—at least not inside our house. She stays outside, especially because of what she did to Jad.

Like any little boy of three or four, Jad at one time spent a fair amount of time in tears. He bit his tongue, or got spanked, or teased, or fell down. And if it hurt enough he cried.

When Jad cried, Gypsy got very nervous. She would skitter around, scrunch up her body, lay back her ears, and appear to have lost whatever minimal sense cats possess.

Then, one day she went berserk.

Jad was flopped on his back, writhing and wailing over some discipline or deprivation, and Gypsy was on the opposite side of the room, pacing. The next instant, Gypsy had sprung clear across the room and attacked Jad, digging both her teeth and claws deep into his face. By sheer grace, I was already in the room, and within seconds pulled the cat off him.

Now I went berserk, torn momentarily between either dispatching the cat with a swift kick to the head or tending to Jad's sickening face wounds.

I tended Jad, while other members of the family tumbled into the room, drawn by his agonized cries of pain and my roars of outrage.

Gypsy slunk into a corner.

I screamed for someone to get that cat out of here, permanently. Alison scurried to remove Gypsy from the house.

Gypsy had really hurt Jad; a full set of teeth marks was visible high on his cheek, piercing the skin already being stretched by swelling flesh. The other cheek was rent with jagged streaks where one set of claws had plowed a course from ear to lip. Another set of claws had been embedded in his shoulder.

When I saw that Jad's eyes were not damaged and that, though very painful, his wounds were shallow and not serious, my thoughts flitted back to the cat. I would destroy her.

Somehow, Jad sensed my feeling.

The attack had occurred no more than three minutes before and he was still crying, his face bloody and his flesh yet untreated. But he must have seen the murderous glint in my eye.

His response, delivered through sobs, floored me: "Alison loves Gypsy so much. I don't care if she does it again. But please don't get rid of her. Alison would be so sad."

Incredible. He doesn't care if Gypsy attacks him again, so long as his sister doesn't lose her beloved pet.

I was stunned by his words and felt such a flood of tenderness toward him that I turned back to dressing his wounds, deferring Gypsy's fate. How she was eventually banished to the out of doors, never to enter the house again, is of little consequence.

But I was indelibly impressed by the depth of caring that is latent between brothers and sisters. Beneath all the squabbling and jealousy and teasing that ricochet around the house, a fierce bond of loyalty is vibrant there. It takes only an attack on one to animate it in the others.

I felt it when I was a child, too. I was about four the night that Jay, then six, wasn't home before dark. Increasingly worried speculation passed above me between my mother and father. Finally, my father resolved to take the car and search for him. I was permitted to accompany him, although I did so fearfully. The concern and anger on his face were difficult to decipher; I could not predict what was going to happen when we found Jay.

He was found watching a bonfire. With a firm, fiercely quiet voice, my father told him to get into the car. We rode home in terrifying silence.

I was sent into the house, and Jay was led to the garage. My father removed his belt.

In seconds, Jay's cries carried across the yard and into the house. "Stop it," I yelled. "Stop it! Stop it! STOP IT!"

Maybe we were never closer than that night. Far past bedtime, we lay awake in the dark, feeling sorry for ourselves and each other. We marveled that we had survived the onslaught of that angry ogre.

And now my children yell "Stop it!" at me, when this ogre deals smartly with a brother or sister. They yell at me, or make menacing gestures, or threaten to run away. And I feel good about it.

Because I suspect that the impulses of caring that brothers and sisters feel for each other are the source of other kinds of caring.

Caring about friends and their feelings. About classmates without friends. About people they know, and people they do not know.

I want my children to feel other people's pain, and to respond to the impulse to stand with them in their pain. I want them to feel upset when the hungry go without food and the homeless go without warmth and the hopeless go without anyone.

But the time of my children's lives seems designed to blunt their natural capacity for empathy with those who suffer. Take TV. Research now indicates that children's constant exposure to violence on television, whether fictional or news, prompts them to distance themselves from either empathy or involvement. Who can blame them? To have witnessed some ten or twelve *thousand* deaths on TV, as the typical teenager will have, justifies some defense against personal pain, the same way my mind glazes over any effort to feel a real sense of Belsen and Dachau.

And so I cherish their capacity to feel each other's pain. It is a sign of life. I don't know how to nurture it, or even if that's possible. I may be able to help preserve it, though, by keeping them from immersion in the tidal wave of TV carcasses.

It's possible, too, that I can personally represent it, by involving them in some of the ways I try to create change in our world. They can learn that a person's work is purposeful, as well as productive. Sometimes simultaneously, and sometimes at the cost of apparent productivity.

But they're going to have to decide whether they'll *basically* be givers or takers. There can be pain either way, but the pain of the takers is personal and pointless. The pain of the givers is corporate and pointed.

And where there is no shared pain, there is no family, much less the family of man.

AFTER SIX MONTHS OF THIS REFLECTING ON THE PROCESS of my life in this family, there is one kind of pain I am no closer to understanding than I was on New Year's Day. I am not even sure who experiences it most acutely—me, Patti, the children (now or later) . . . ?

I become more aware of it at this time, when school lets out. Patti and the children are home a lot now and the volume of everyday tasks and interactions seems to increase. So, in some ways, does the tension.

# THE RELUCTANT DRAGOON
## *or*

### *JUST ANOTHER FOOTSOLDIER IN THE HOUSEHOLD ARMY*

I CAN MAKE MY WAY ALL RIGHT IN MOST ORGANIZATIONS. If I'm managing an operation, I can pretty well see what needs to be done, and delegate the tasks. If I'm in a sub-management position, I can do support work with some enthusiasm. And as a consultant or a board member, my sporadic contributions have been of some value.

I am no whiz-bang executive, mind you, and the corporate headhunters are not clamoring to bid for my body. But I know the good feeling of being in charge, and being competent to anticipate and handle most of what needs to be done in most organizations.

My family, however, is not such an organization. It is as though I check my brains at the door when I walk into the house. If I don't exactly feel like a peon, I feel like a board member who has a hazy sense of the daily priorities and policies of operating management. I know I am responsible, but I am clearly not in charge.

I think Patti is in charge.

In any case, I sense that she carries in her head an interminable list of tasks great and small which are essential if our household is to function. Car pool schedules, birthday gift procurement, laundry at home and dry cleaning downtown, rabies boosters for the dogs, burial for the latest deletion from the children's pet menagerie of fish, snakes, mice, hermit crabs, cats, dogs, birds, *et al.*, library books to return, costumes for the ballet recital, adult social calendar, children's social calendar, light bulb replacements, automobile inspection, parental visits, arrangements for feeding pets and watering plants during a weekend trip—not to mention clear glass and green glass recycling on the first and third Wednesdays, newspaper bundling and pickup on second and fourth Wednesdays, garbage cans put out every Wednesday and Saturday, and sporadic clean-up weeks when bagged leaves and bundled clippings cut to 36 inches are to be put at the curb.

There is more, of course. But I don't want to think of all those details. In fact, I cannot think of them all.

And so, when I come into the house, I need to be told what to do.

I don't much like that, and I put up with it only because I recognize the necessity of keeping ahead of the surge of things to be done. Certainly, it's not fair to Patti to let her do it all—that senseless, repetitious cafeteria of tasteless tasks—nor is it fair that she must become straw boss and chief nag. I *ought* to be able to help take charge. But, for some reason, I cannot.

I don't think I enjoy feeling like a dolt. But I become so uninspired by the catalog of chores that I have settled for the lot of quietly churlish serf, waiting to be told where to hoe next.

That can't be too good for the children. I'd rather they saw their father as an enthusiastic co-manager, eager to do the tasks of our daily life together.

But all they get is me, hiding out in the john with a magazine, until my guilt level impels me to conjure up some trivial chore I can initiate before someone tells me what to do.

The project is usually good for about three minutes. Then it's right back to tell-me-what-I-can-do-to-help.

How can I be so active, so initiating, in every other realm of my life, and still be so passive about household affairs? Where does that dichotomy stem from?

Not from my own father. He always had a ready list of things which he pitched into with some enthusiasm. And I don't think I was conscripted so often that I turned sour on those tasks out of lingering resentment.

The only thing I like less than being that way is not knowing why I am.

SUMMER HAS BROUGHT A DELICIOUS LULL IN THE PACE OF my daily work, and I find more of my energies focussed on writing. Perhaps what I wind up with will really be a book.

I feel self-conscious about that possibility. After all, I don't really presume that my personal, subjective reflections are just what every other father—who has his own—is waiting for.

In fact, I hope just the opposite.

# I DON'T WANT TO KNOW

### *or*

### KEEPING THE EXPERTS
### FROM MAKING YOU A STRANGER
### TO YOUR CHILDREN

THEY HAVE PROLIFERATED LIKE HOMESPUN BUNNIES SINCE
World War II. Every week a new one is proclaimed
champion counsel for the needy. They fill shelf after
shelf in the bookstores. There's nearly always one on
the best-seller list. Excerpts grace the pages of all the
leading monthlies and every self-respecting Sunday
newspaper supplement.

They are the books on child-rearing.

They are enough to make you seek retroactive celi-
bacy.

All manner of men and women have taken to print
during the Age of Psychology to share their expertise
with us who shape the succeeding generations. All have
a finding, or a viewpoint, or a shard of truth about the
way little humans develop. Further, most have some
keen sense of how we must go about parenting our chil-

dren to maximize their potential, minimize their traumas, optimize their ego-development.

And all that sort of stuff.

Of which I weary. And, when I'm not *too* weary, I get angry about it. For some of these people who are knowledgeable about children seem to have promoted themselves into a place no parent should let them occupy—that of seeming to know better than the parent does what is best for a particular child, in a particular family situation.

It takes ludicrous forms. A typically anxious suburban parent told me of great gratitude and frustration over a best-selling book on parent-child relations. The gratitude was boundless, for the book supplied appropriate parental responses for at least a few thousand probable inquiries. This parent mastered them all, and felt equipped if not competent to handle a child's questions.

Hence, the bottomless frustration. The parent had "tried everything I could think of," but couldn't get the child to ask a single damned one of the right questions.

All dressed up, and nowhere to go. And nobody to go with. For that parent and child are on different trips, on which they may or may not chance to meet. The parent's itinerary was set by this great cartographer of juvenile psyches. The *child's* itinerary emerges out of intensely personal daily urges and interactions.

One of those interactions will be the one with this encyclopedically remote parent who will eventually communicate a lot of unintended things to that child.

One result, for the child, is likely to be a sense of the parent's earnest ineptitude. Another will be the conclusion that childhood is infinitely complicated and the parenting task is dreadfully likely to come a cropper. What else could justify these parental preparations rivaling the reflex conditioning and memorization of emergency procedures undertaken by astronauts?

That's a crummy impression for a kid to get—the suspicion that his parents don't know—in their guts—what to do with him.

And a lot of that erosion of parental confidence is a by-product of the incessant tidal waves of popular psychology. "At last!", begins the advertising copy, "*the* commonsense way for parents to . . ."

And I keep wishing the "at last" were really true, knowing all the while that here is a literary exercise in which an infinite number of "laters" will always come after "last." Each will contribute to the impression that children are perfectible, if only parents would perfectly practice one method or another.

And the descending spiral continues dispiritedly. We see "imperfections" in our children, and assume inadequacy in ourselves, for not having prevented these "flaws." Not only do we not know innately what is best for our children, the beat goes on, but we can't even follow the clear instructions of experts. Woe to us.

Rubbish! And robbery!

Robbery of intimacy and spontaneity and warmth and hurt and forgiveness and trial and error and trust in the toughness of our children and ourselves.

What a child needs to know is that his parents want him, like him, will do what they can to help him find his way as a once-in-eternity creation with gifts we wait hopefully to see unfold among us. He needs to know that the unfolding is not dependent upon his perfection, and may in fact arise in the midst or wake of a "flaw" in his life. He needs to know that the unfolding is not dependent upon his parents' perfect parenting of him, and may in fact be powered by the energy of his coping with their imperfection.

Trust life.

That comes first. Trust life. *Then* check out a book or two on what makes it tick, if you're so inclined. I am not, after all, pro-ignorance when it comes to child-rearing. I consider myself widely read, and reasonably well read, in the field. I have done course work, work-shops, parent-training groups—the whole shot. I have learned a lot, and my children have certainly benefited from what I have learned.

But it took a while before I realized that looking be-yond myself for understanding about children required some perspective, lest it cut two ways—both equally unpromising. Children could begin to appear infinitely complicated and fragile, making them somewhat strange. And my native instincts could be shelved in favor of book learning, making me somewhat of a stranger.

When we were young parents and avid students of literature about children, Patti summed it all up one evening: "Too much education sure can make you tense."

Tense is a strange way to be, about something so natural as parenting.

I don't want to be a stranger to my children, or vice versa. I want them to know that I trust their life-force to withstand the vagaries of my parenting. I want them to see me in action, in my life, and I want to see them in action in theirs. We can compare notes. What works? What doesn't? Who said what that hurt, or healed? When wasn't something fair? Who was courageous?

I think the children are more interested in knowing my commitments, than in being parented professionally.

Did I want them? Do I like them? Do I trust them? Once they know the answers to those questions, they want to touch other sinews in me.

Like my convictions.

Am I a giver or a taker, in the commerce of humanity? Am I generous, or niggardly? How consistently do I put myself in front selfishly? Dynamically? Reluctantly? How do I value people? Discredit them? What will I put up with, and why, and for how long?

Will my way work for them?

My father took me with him sometimes when he went to inspect the construction of houses he designed. One day—I was perhaps ten—we entered a nearly completed home perched dramatically on the crown of a high hill overlooking San Francisco Bay. Dad's contemporary design thrilled and impressed me—redwood beams and panels framing huge windows, contrasting with occasional white plaster walls. One such wall stood between the living and dining rooms.

On Dad's plans, the opening had square corners, of course, in keeping with the contemporary lines of the house. In reality, as we stood there, some gratuitous corrupter had rounded off the corners, creating a 1930s style archway in the wall.

My father was calm but steeped in ominous purposefulness as he went about undoing the wrong which had been committed. He walked outside to the construction scrap heap and found a four-foot length of Orangeburg pipe—the fat, pebbly, cast-iron kind used for sewage lines. With measured steps, he carried it back into the house on his shoulder, like a bazooka.

Or a baseball bat. For he walked up to the wall, took a Babe Ruth stance before the offending arch, sized it up for a moment, and then battered the wall to smithereens.

Not in a frenzy. Carefully, patiently, like a seasoned woodsman felling a tree. He let the weight of the Orangeburg do the work. Crunch. Stroke. Crunch. Stroke. Crunch. The plaster clattered to the floor. Two-by-fours splintered and nails screeched as they were twisted from their lodging. Electric junction boxes crumpled and wires sagged in space, with nowhere to go.

After a while, Dad was through.

Almost. He put down the pipe and took one of his oblong, flat-leaded pencils from his pocket and found the largest piece of plaster. On it, he wrote a message to the contractor. It had something to do with vandalism.

The contractor, he said, was a vandal.

I learned a lot about my father that day. About my father, and about life. About right and wrong and integrity and a host of things no book could have ever told him how to teach me.

I'm sure he never read a book on child-rearing. And perhaps if he had he might have been more understanding and done some things, or not done some things, that would have spared me later pain. But those pains I have coped with, one way or another.

And I still have all the benefits of life with a man to whom I was no puzzle to be pieced together, and who was no stranger to me. I knew the sinews of his life. I have chosen freely and frequently from what that man let me see of him living his life, and they are the themes of enduring power in my own.

Now if I can infuse my presence among my children with an informed understanding of them, without contaminating us both, then I will have built and improved upon the design my father passed on.

And I will be no vandal, either.

MY FATHER HAD FAIRLY UNCOMPLICATED IDEAS ABOUT how to spend our vacations. That's one area where I have chosen to be quite different from him. My ideas are not necessarily complicated, but how we handle them surely is.

Most summers we have traveled far from home. Our destination is decided in a reasonably democratic process, wherein the children suggest options, calculate costs, weigh benefits and sometimes mourn lost causes, just as Patti and I do. Making up our common mind about how we'll spend our vacation is one of our more egalitarian family exercises. It is not always thus when it comes to family decision-making.

# "BUT IT'S NOT FAIR!"
## *or*

### DECIDING WHEN DEMOCRACY YIELDS TO BENEVOLENT DESPOTISM—OR EVEN TO ARBITRARY DICTATORSHIP

WHEN THE WORDS ARE SPOKEN CHILD TO CHILD, THEY ARE blunt and angry: "That's not fair!"

They assert a stance, a judgment, a right. They are a challenge to a peer, and an insistence that things be settled equitably. The challenger has some confidence that justice can be wrought without any adult help.

But when the line is intended for a parent's ears, they take on an entirely different inflection and meaning. The last word is tortured into about three syllables, all braided through a dissonant whine: "But it's not faaaaaaaaaaayuherrrrrrrr!"

I hear that a lot.

And, on occasion, I learn a lot when I listen. It *wasn't* fair that our oldest child wound up with most of the money-earning opportunities around the house. We had just fallen into the habit of turning to her first.

Nor was it fair that younger children wound up with more hand-me-downs—or with fewer household responsibilities. And so the chorus of complaint wafts plaintively through the house from time to time, and I do the best I can to arbitrate or explain or comfort.

And I do tolerably well when I have to settle accounts between children, or even modify a parental policy of dividing assets and liabilities.

I come unglued, though, at the suggestion that things ought to be equally divided between children and parents.

"How come you and Mom have the only bedroom with a bath in the house?"

What shameless temerity! What disrespect! Don't they understand parental prerogatives? Just who do they think they are, anyhow?

"Well, why do you?"

The question does not go away just because it is cheeky, and my children are not inclined to be pointlessly smartass. There's a rudimentary sense of dignity and self-respect which makes the asking of the question reasonable, and so I begin to wonder just who they really do think they are.

I like what I conclude, because they aren't really seeking undifferentiated status between adults and children. Quite the opposite.

The asking does not anticipate our eventual eviction from our bedroom. I think they really want to know, from time to time, the remaining distinctions between children and adults. They feel themselves growing at a somewhat breathtaking clip, assuming increasing responsibilities, and they see themselves being plunged headlong into adulthood by rock music and Madison Avenue and full-breasted Barbie dolls.

They are asking, "What's left of childhood?"

And they hope the answer is, "Plenty."

They *are* still children. And I want them to know that. And, until they are adults, we who are will exercise some parental prerogatives.

One of them is assigning to ourselves the bedroom-with-bath in our house. Others include making some less-than-democratic decisions about a whole covey of affairs, from bedtime to practice schedules for piano, to allowances, to church participation.

I do listen to their opinions, and to their feelings. But decisions are not made by consensus, in matters where their development as children is concerned. In the matters where they are clearly *children*, the adults will decide.

There are other kinds of questions that clearly invite consensus, like how we will spend our vacation. I see no reason why a matter of pleasure should be decided without regard for what everyone considers fun.

I used to wish my own father felt that way.

From Fresno, you could go two hours east or two hours west and be in equally magnificent places—the High Sierras and the Monterey coast. All my friends and their families went west, to the beaches of Monterey and Carmel and Santa Cruz. How gloriously their vacation days passed.

—Screaming, whirling, slamming rides on the carnival machinery. I liked them all. Except the roller coaster, of course. Only after you were staggering down the exit ramp did you discover the cotton candy had been clenched into a confectionary Brillo pad.

—Slow motion days basking in the sun on a tiny beach next to the best hamburger stand on the California coastline, for refueling between surfing forays or card games or volleyball.

—Wide-eyed rides along Seventeen Mile Drive at Pebble Beach, craning for glimpses of the rich whose palaces lined the way, and dreaming of the day of possession . . .

But the Daleys went east, to the mountains, and watched my father fish.

Year after year.

Boring? Boring!! Do you have *any* idea what it's like to be the only kid your age at Sheep Creek campground in Sequoia National Park? Year after year? Words fail me.

So I do not ask my children to accompany me on a trip to do what gives pleasure only to me. Vacations we decide by consensus.

But bedrooms, I assign. And I believe they want it that way. Something comes over them, after the customary reflex reaction against my acting "bossy." It is a calm, a sense of security.

It must be a comfortable feeling to know that someone *is* taking care of you, even in ways that may rankle for a while. A child must feel good to understand that a parent knows more than the child, and is stronger and wiser in some ways—competent to frame directions for growing.

They know I don't perpetuate their childhood. And when I inadvertently stunt their growth, they let me know rather forcefully. But I do want to create a space, by my exercise of prerogative, where they can grow at their own pace, savoring the uniqueness of these days, relaxing in the knowledge that they do have a father who can take care of them.

It will not always be thus.

My father died, and so will theirs. And eventually they will have to take care of others, with no recourse to another. I see them practicing now, by healing dolls and disciplining pets and staging backyard festivals to raise money for the hungry.

My exercise of parental prerogative doesn't seem to deflate their personal sense of responsibility. Paradoxically, it may be a fostering influence, letting them lay claim to it at their own pace, while providing some kind of model of a grown-up who likes being responsible.

Yes, I think that's coming along all right.

Now I wonder if they know how much I miss my father, and how much I would like to be taken care of sometimes.

THE VACATION DECISION HAS BEEN FITLY MADE. NEXT month we'll be off—loafing and sailing and reading and writing on a small island we all decided should be our summer nesting ground for the years ahead. And now, just a few weeks before we leave, I will once again take a swat at dieting away the roundness that cleverly disguises my admirable physique just beneath.

Lots of luck.

# DON'T DO AS I DID;
# DO AS I SAY

*or*

## TRYING TO DO RIGHT BY YOUR CHILD
## BY DOING THE OPPOSITE
## OF WHAT YOUR PARENTS DID

I WAS DETERMINED NOT TO REPEAT MY PARENTS' MISTAKE.

I refused to stand idly by and watch one of my own children become pudgy. I plotted and executed a forceful intervention, powered by sour childhood memories of my lonely and furtive snatching at food.

"You will jog with me," I declared.

"If you think I'm going to go out and run around the stupid high school and work up a gross sweat like you do," she replied, "you're cracked."

In fact, I felt cracked.

I had never before attempted to *force* a child to do something, just by sheer bullying. But I was prepared to make an exception. She might not want to jog, but being pudgy was no treat, either. Given a choice between having a bully for a father or a bulge for a stomach, I was prepared to make the decision for her.

"You will jog with me," I repeated.

"Dad, be reasonable. What will the kids think if they see me galloping around the track in an ugly sweat suit?"

I did not feel reasonable. I felt fanatic. The campaign began. I hammered on her. I anesthetized all my concern for her reactions and rights. I had a cause, and I would prevail.

I would save her from the squalid joys of furtive overeating. I knew them well. Filching a quarter to buy a box of cookies to tastelessly massacre while locked in the bathroom—only to discover that the empty container wouldn't flush down the toilet.

What *do* you do with a wet Nabisco box?

Whatever those times may have gained me as an exercise in resourcefulness was more than lost in other, ego-staining ways.

But my parents never seemed to notice. Their growing boy's growth was fairly well out of control, but the subject was never mentioned. Not once. Until, at age fourteen, I exploded at dinner one night and begged for some help in controlling myself. Their genuine surprise at my concern only magnified my rage at these mindless accomplices who had abandoned me to my problem.

I swore I would never make that mistake with my own children. And so I finally bludgeoned my daughter into submission. She began to jog with me.

Once she had surrendered, she looked for ways to make the experience tolerable. First, it was the challenge of working up to a mile. But that took only a week. Next, it was trying for two miles. But that took more effort than a surly conscript was prepared to exert, and by the end of the second week, we were in trouble.

Every morning began with a fight. She refused to come jog. I told her she would come if I had to carry her to the track and boot her around it. And I really meant it.

She may hate me for it now, I told myself, but someday she'll be grateful.

I was right about the first part.

We became enemies.

Real enemies. The lifelong fund of friendliness between us withered and disappeared. All that remained was my fanatical mission and its would-be sacrificial lamb, scared and struggling to escape.

Finally I couldn't stand it anymore. Whatever error of omission my parents may have committed, it never cost so dearly as this crusade.

I apologized to her, and we became friends again.

That was all I cared about, and the incident was forgotten. But I still puzzled, occasionally, at my abandonment of all sense of proportion, and at how powerful were the forces of reaction against my parents' passivity.

I couldn't do what they did, but I couldn't do the opposite, either. Nor was I rational enough to find a middle way. And although the jogging fiasco foreclosed any further direct intervention on my daughter's behalf, I felt sorry she would have to go the rotund route I had taken.

One more mistake. She had plans of her own, which is to say a life of her own. And six months later, for reasons and rhythms private within her, she undertook an unobtrusive shape-up campaign, melting away what separates soft little girls from shapely young ladies.

It is not her problem any more.

Probably, it never was. It is so easy to implicate the children in my own needs, using them to bolster my resolve or to justify my weakness. Better be more discriminating about how they are like me, and where the limits of commonality lie. And I will be, for their sakes.

I had just hoped to have someone with whom I could share my problem.

ALL OF US GOT AWAY ON VACATION RIGHT ON SCHEDULE. The only hitch is that all of *me* came along. My shape-up campaign needs some shaping up.

This island, however, is all I dreamed of. I am spending most mornings writing these thoughts, and most afternoons sailing. Woven throughout it all are Patti and Alison and Shannon and Jad, in a seemingly endless ripple of pleasant interplay with no agenda.

With no bridges, no roads, and no commercial ferry access to this place, the water is a friendly moat. It holds in abeyance the tide of busy-ness which surges against us the rest of the year.

In the space it creates, we find friends—within the family, and beyond.

And we ask old questions.

# "HOW MUCH MONEY DO YOU MAKE, DADDY?"

*or*

## TRYING TO REFLECT LASTING VALUES TO YOUR CHILDREN

WHEN I MADE UP THE LIST OF SUBJECTS I WANTED TO write about, most of them were pretty fresh. Shannon had just asked me, for instance, how much money I make.

But that was almost a year ago, and so I have wondered from time to time whether this particular subject is still worth discussing. As I made my morning coffee today, before coming out here on the porch to write this chapter, the improbable happened—Alison asked me how much money I make.

The subject, obviously, endures.

But why did this child ask me this question today? And why did I hedge my answer, as I did when Shannon asked, and finally duck the question altogether?

I think I know why she asked the question. We are

presently on vacation, comfortably settled on a coastal island in Maine. We have been here a week now, with three more to follow.

The island is an enchanted 500-acre jumble of rocks and pines and blueberries and meadows, planted firmly in the waters of Sheepscot Bay. Tucked in amid the flora and fauna native to the island are thirty or so families of human beings—summer people.

They are our new peer group, and I think the children want to know where we fit in, how we rank in this new society. Back home they have all that pretty well worked out. But this is new territory, with an established pecking order to fit into.

Right off the bat, they know we are second-class citizens of a sort.

We rent.

Worse, this is our first year here, although we are quick to point out to anyone who will feign listening that we spent Thanksgiving week here with owner-friends. And we fully expect, twenty years from now, to be twenty-year veterans of summer on the island.

But for now, we are somewhat lacking in substance and local pedigree. So the kids are working it out as best they can, trying to get bearings on how to regard themselves vis-à-vis their peers. We don't own, but the house we rent is a prize. We are new, but with honorable intentions. We are renting sailboats this summer, but we own a nice old classic motor launch. We get extra points because it is wooden.

The kids know we are not the richest people on the island. By a long shot. They see the anchorage studded with magnificent craft twice the size and thirty times the price of ours, and even my seven-year-old son has become adept at reading the horsepower ratings on the sides of outboard motors as launches and runabouts bounce and skim past our porch. If 40 h.p. is good, then 65 h.p. must be better. Lucky people.

If some houses are comfortably splendid, others exude a rustic magnificence. Even in Paradise, I suppose, there are good addresses.

The question this morning came from a more direct source of comparison, though. Last night Alison had accompanied me to the home of a longtime cottage-owning sailboat owner. We were going there to negotiate the charter of his sailboat. She sat patiently as he and I sipped our drinks on his porch, getting acquainted. Our host was an engaging and enthusiastic man who, in affirming his affection for his work, volunteered that he would happily take a ten-thousand-dollar-a-year pay cut and still feel lucky.

"Well then," she pursued this morning, "if you won't tell me how much you make, tell me this: If you made ten thousand dollars less, could we still live on it?"

I smiled with a wan nonchalance and supposed we could. Satisfied, she went on with breakfast.

Disturbed, I came out here to write.

What is all this malarkey about masking income? Why can't I just give her a straight answer to a straight question?

For a couple of reasons.

I used to think it was to diminish the importance of money. But now I doubt that is a reason at all.

The least honest real reason is that I don't know for sure, since my income fluctuates with the fortunes of my various activities.

What's harder to write, and therefore probably closer to the truth, is that I can create an expandable illusion by withholding specifics—giving the children room to magnify their father's wealth and worth.

But if I say I make so many thousand dollars a year, I am pegged, right there. There is no chance my children will take me for a two-hundred-thousand-a-year man—or a closet millionaire.

And I'd like to be taken for either or both, more than I care to admit. More than I'd care to admit, because neither has anything to do with what animates my life. Hence, this stupid conflict, as contradictory as it is persistent: Don't tell the kids how much you make for fear they'll reduce their regard, all the while wanting them to know that the value of life is unrelated to the purchase price of anything.

Worth is utterly other than net worth.

The vexation is compounded by my being my father's son. A largely self-taught architect, he made precious little money during his professional career, oscillating between stints of utterly impecunious independent practice, and several short-lived partnerships. These ventures provided relatively steady streams of modest income.

They also entailed an immoderate amount of conflict between my father and his growing roster of former partners. He was, I gather, no simple joy to work with. He wanted to do things the right way, as distinct from what he perceived as the short-cut methods of lesser men. And so, with some regularity, he would pack up his integrity and move his practice back into a spare room at home—there to wait for a client, who rarely thought to look for him in such a place.

All those years, I wished deeply that he made more money. All my friends' fathers did, and I wanted mine to do so too. I did not like his work style. I did not respect it.

I did not understand it.

But now I do, and so I am torn between the hollow momentum of a longstanding desire to have more money, and the quiet determination to live my life my way—a way that does not require more money, a way which may even be jeopardized by it.

The conflict contaminates the answers my children get, or do not get.

Perhaps the next time a child asks me a simple question, I can provide a simple answer. Let them make of it what they will. If I am judged by the answer I give, I will be at least equally judged by the way I give it. And that matters more.

After all, it's their sense of *value* I care about.

OUR TIME TOGETHER HERE HAS HAD INFINITE VALUE. IN a little while, it will be over. We'll run the last boat-load of bags to the mainland dock, there to pack them in our station wagon which is covered with a month's dust. I'll tell Bill Plummer that he can haul our boat to the shed for winter storage. Then I'll go to Ray Grover's general store to settle our account for the summer, tell Mr. and Mrs. Thibodeaux we'll miss their lobsters, climb into our car, buckle up, and drive away.

As the three shops of the village and dozen boats in the small harbor recede in my rear view mirror, I will feel profoundly sad.

I will begin to miss my children.

Oh, we're all going home together all right. But it will be different, at home. And I am not sure it will be different for the better.

# THE GREAT JUGGLING ACT
### *or*
## TRYING TO DO JUSTICE TO BOTH A CAREER AND A FAMILY

I HAVE HEARD A LOT, LATELY, ABOUT HOW DIFFICULT IT is for a woman to juggle both a career and her parenting responsibilities. One or the other is bound to suffer. And when something has to give, it is usually the career. Many women are angry about that and a bunch of men and children may be catching hell because of it.

That is genuinely too bad. We *ought* to be partners in the struggle. Because, speaking as one of the men-folk, I claim to know how that conflict feels, to be torn between career and family. Women may be tired of being regarded, culturally, as housekeepers and diaper washers; well, I'm tired of being culturally regarded as a breadwinner whose prime responsibility to the family is to be a "good provider."

Meaning money.

When will anyone get around to noticing that some of us men yearn to matter more, in this what-do-you-do? (and I-wonder-what-he-makes?) rat race.

I'd rather be a father.

I do extraordinarily interesting things in my work. I really love it. And I earn plenty enough to get by. But I'd rather be a father. I care more about how my children emerge than I do about how big my business gets and what numbers appear on the bottom line.

That doesn't make me the forerunner of a new breed of American males, I suppose, but neither does it make me a freak.

We talk frequently, friends and I. Some say it right away; others only let clues slip, once they feel safe. But their message is the same: work matters most mostly by default. If I knew, they say, any way to let something else matter more, I would in an instant. But work is where I get a paycheck, and that matters. Work is where I get a report card, and that matters. Work is where I have a place—defined and reserved for me—and that matters.

None of those are silly or invalid reasons. They just aren't ultimately important, except in a vacuum.

Yet a vacuum is what exists for fathers who want to devote themselves to fathering with the same intensity that would be considered natural and normal for a mother. Where is the support for a father who wants to take off to go with his child's class on a field trip? Who will congratulate the man who trims his chances for advancement by refusing to bring home a full briefcase every night or to move every two years or to commute himself to death? Who will hug the man who aches to weep for the futility of such busy-ness, and then to emerge from the grief content to be a father?

I will.

And surprisingly others will, too. Like an underground resistance recognizing a password, some people close at hand will eagerly whisper their complicity in this common yearning to be natural and normal.

Rather than average.

A long-distance runner from the Ozarks taught me that difference, between normal and average. It's normal, he reminded me, for the human body to be able to run ten or fifteen miles without caving in. The fact that most men can't go a couple of hundred yards without wheezing is merely average. And average, he went on, is no way to gauge yourself. Normal's what you've got to find, and then get there.

I'm beginning to sense what is normal for me. Certainly it is not wanting to be more into my children's lives and games. It is for *my* life to be more available to my children, in virtually any realm of activity. To enable them to find out anything they want to know about me at work, for instance. What I do. How I treat people. How I plan and execute jobs. How I handle pressure. What I get out of it.

Or to involve them in any decision-making that affects them—and even some that doesn't, just because I value their opinions. Or to be honest with them about family tensions that may be in the air, and exchange candid feedback about how we're living our life together.

It is also normal for me to want to see any of my children in any kind of performance they give, from classroom bathrobe drama to neighborhood magic show to piano recital. I'll change travel schedules, postpone appointments, and leave overlong meetings before they are concluded, just to be there. Not average, I'll grant, but normal for me.

That's the easy part, though, something like getting to the performances. But all that other stuff I said was normal, I don't do that yet. I *want* to. I just don't.

I write about it, instead. There's at least a little adult status in that, you know.

Back to square number one: how do I justify channeling a major thrust of my life into fathering, when so little around me—so little of all that is average—supports it? How can I sweep away all that average clutter, to let the normal be known? Why do I let myself be nudged away from what I know to be important, in favor of what is merely urgent?

Important lasts and lasts; urgent, by definition, dies in a hurry. I do not want to burn up my life tending urgent little brush fires. And still I can't push myself over the edge. Yet. I continue to chart my worth by beacons and landmarks set out by average men, to be followed by men like me who are persistently more average than normal.

Incredible. True, but incredible. I mean, what have I done in my whole life that was of any more significance than fathering three human beings. Once they were not—didn't exist. Now they live, the fruit of our love. They have independent lives, they hurt and heal and love and laugh, they make mistakes and weave magic, they will bear children and celebrate and mourn . . .

That counts. Ultimately. I know it does, and I am determined to give my fathering its due. But I can't help wishing for some help, something we men could do for each other to support our being normal.

Like, I wish someone had given a baby shower for *me*, too.

I BEGIN THE AUTUMN SURGE WITH NEW DETERMINATION to keep my priorities in order. Everything seems to start—or to start over—in September. I am launched on an exhilarating new round of projects in my work. Patti has returned to her work, enjoying the fruits of some careful team-building done last year among the specialized staff. Alison, Shannon, and Jad all seem well pleased with their teachers and classmates, within normal limits. The pace quickens for us all.

I feel buoyed, too, by the time on the island. There is a fund of feeling between us all that built up there and has not been obliterated yet.

I am determined that it won't be, either.

But the tasks of living together in the months ahead are so very different from those of the month just past. So are the outside influences.

# IF IT WAS
# GOOD ENOUGH FOR ME . . .
## *or*
## INSTITUTING AN EFFECTIVE PROGRAM OF BENIGN DEPRIVATION

IT IS ONLY SEPTEMBER, BUT ALREADY THE CHILDREN ARE watching the mailbox for the Christmas catalogs. We also know they are due any day, and if we can beat the kids to the mailbox, we can hide them away for a month or two.

A month or two of peace and quiet.

For the moment these colorful literary hucksters begin to pass from hand to hand, inflaming juvenile acquisitive passions, we know there will be instant erosion of whatever self-reliance and self-restraint we've intermittently thought to encourage in our young. The "want" lists will be prepared with infinite care and presented by each, in his or her own inimitable style.

Alison goes for written hints.

I grope my way out of bed in the dawn dimness, groggy but anxious to keep an early morning tennis date. I shuffle across the bedroom to the vanity, lean over, splash a little water on my face, feel around for a towel, cover my dripping face, and straighten up. As I draw the towel down from my brow to below my eyes a small patch appears on the mirror before me. I lean closer. It is a printed blur. I find my glasses.

It is a clipping, taped on my mirror by a late-night elf:

> *Arabian Horse,* The Magazine for Enthusiasts. Enjoy a full year's subscription for only $35. Bonus: Subscribe now and get the Arabian Breeders Directory free. Added extra bonus:
> Enclose full payment with your order and receive free Arabian Horse Lover's Calendar, with full-color pictures. Makes a wonderful gift.

The last sentence is underlined in Magic Marker. I could see that even without my glasses.

In due time, we will find Alison's full list, offered up in installments, variously taped, tacked, glued, propped and magnetically clipped all over 159 Hickory Court. In all, she will request about four times what she expects to get, to give us a little latitude in selection. And, perhaps, a little inducement to go overboard.

She takes care to ensure that each installment has received notice: "Isn't it incredible the way those new fiberglass skis are so light, compared to the old metal ones?"

"What are you talking about?"

"The skis. Didn't you see the thing on your dashboard?"

"What thing?"

"The folder on the skis. I got it down at Varsity Sports. I thought you'd want to see it—all about fiberglass skis. Christmas is coming you know. With snow, remember? Remember snow?"

I remember.

"And remember the promise you made when you sold the camping trailer—that the money would go for skis for all of us?"

I do remember, but would rather not. I had long since spent the money on brickwork for our entry courtyard.

"But," she continues, "I suppose you have long since spent the money on landscaping or some dumb thing like that."

"Well . . ."

"So the least you could do would be to think about skis for Christmas. That's why the brochure is on your dashboard."

"I'll give it a look."

Shannon is just the opposite. She probably spends just about as much time leafing through catalogs and smudging up shop windows along Nassau Street. But she is much more demure in the communication of her desires.

I ask Patti, as the fall wears on and the holidays approach, "What do you suppose Shannon wants for Christmas?"

"More than anything, I think, she'd like to have a shaggy rug for her bedroom."

"Oh, that's right. I remember her saying something about how much difference a rug makes in a room—when we were working on her dollhouse," I reply. "What else?"

"Well, she's beginning to feel a little bit like she has outgrown some of her 'good clothes.' "

"By outgrown, do you mean physically or in terms of just her sense of growing up—that they're too little-girlish."

"The latter."

And so the conversation goes, until we have divined a list of Shannon's wants. And when the list is complete, we are reasonably confident that it encompasses Shannon's heart's desires.

But we are darned if we can figure out how we figured it out.

That's how Shannon communicates such things. Gently. Obliquely. Always allowing room for a free response, pro or con. It is a mode of communication that requires a sensitive listener and observer, and Shannon fortunately has one in Patti.

Patti can register out of the ethers these wispy and evanescent messages and not mistake Shannon's off-handedness for lack of real yearning. She has a gift for hearing not just what is said, but what is meant. She knows that Shannon's take-it-or-leave-it attitude means the parent, not the child, is free to disregard the desire.

A nice pair, those subtle two.

Ain't nothing subtle about Jad though. "Sit down, Dad. I'm going to tell you what to get me for Christmas."

In a trice, I am planted firmly on the sofa in our family room, with a catalog laid in my lap and a son snuggled at my hip.

"Now, this electric racing set is something we could do *together*, Dad."

Subtlety, as I said, is not his long suit.

He knows what he wants, and he makes his wants

known. Before we arise from the sofa, a list will have been written and it will all be over with Jad.

His lists are a bit lengthy, but not altogether unreasonable; no $500 stuffed lions from F. A. O. Schwarz crouching among the hockey sticks and model airplanes.

All the children know that, if they're sensible, there is a strong likelihood that we will buy them most of what they really want. I suppose (but don't tell them) that we could probably buy them all the stuff on their lists if we felt like it.

But for some reason, we don't succumb. No matter how long or short their lists, I feel like *not* buying something—anything—on them, just for the sake of not buying it. The reluctance keeps surfacing in the form of a question: Should any child get everything he asks for?

As nearly as I can make out, it's a question my parents never had to wrestle with. The belt was always pretty tight around the budget when I was growing up. Memories of the milkman standing at the side door, gently badgering Mom for "something on account" are all too clear. If I got an allowance then, I can't remember it now.

Of course I always had the things I really needed, like food and medical care and clothes (albeit hand-me-down or homemade more often than I liked). But the things I *wanted*—a Red Ryder lever-action carbine BB gun complete with leather thong, an .035 gas-powered model airplane, a bicycle, store-bought clothes, and cafeteria-bought-lunches—those things I had to steal, beg, or earn.

I tried all three ways.

I don't know whether stealing or begging was less fun. The stuff I stole I had to think up plausible reasons for possessing, which itself was no problem. It was always easier to justify than to *remember* the story a couple of days later when Mom or Dad would ask, "Now where did you say you got that aviator jacket again?" And in my family, I think it was almost worse to look dumb than to steal . . .

Begging wasn't much better, although I was helped along in ridding myself of the habit. My friends helped, by becoming ex-friends.

So along about age nine or ten, I quit begging for good, quit stealing except for thrills, and began working.

Everything I spent, from age nine or ten on, I earned. I'm not sure in just what ways I'd be different today if that had not been the case, but I know the differences would be profound.

Work became a means to an end—that's how you got what you wanted to buy. (It wasn't supposed to be fun or fulfilling; those notions came later.)

My children don't know that yet, and they may not ever know it just that baldly. They will in early adulthood approach a vocation as a vehicle for self-expression, an opportunity to do something they really enjoy, full of confidence that the pursuit of that self-expression will inevitably yield enough revenue to keep body and soul together.

That's a better way, I have no doubt. I have spent much of my adult life trying to make it true, belatedly, for myself.

So why do I find myself simultaneously wanting to provide them with less than they ask for, to create an artificial deprivation? No parent has to go out of his way to find hassles with his children—why do I pick this issue?

(When my parents didn't get me something, it was

because they couldn't, not because they wouldn't. I hated the circumstances, hated hearing "we can't afford it," but my basic empathy for my parents in our shared circumstances tempered whatever anger I felt at their inability to provide me with what I wanted.)

Like so many parenting decisions, this one seems to hang on autobiographical egocentrism. There is about me some measure of those qualities everyone is supposed to possess and/or admire—self-reliance, resourcefulness, initiative, imagination and responsibility. I don't possess that much of any of those qualities, but I do have some; and what there is, is satisfying. And I think they came from having to work to get what I wanted.

There is something fundamental and healthy about working, about being personally productive, about the satisfactions of achievement. I'm not talking about feeling duty-bound, the result of an artificially induced Protestant work ethic. I see this sense of satisfaction in my children when they proudly present their own paintings, or in the buoyant exhilaration which carried Jad for days when he completed his first model, after a week of intricate effort. Very basic, very natural, very profound, those good feelings. And probably ineradicable.

Even if my children don't like the implication of deprivation, they can at least sense my conviction, when I say, "If it was good enough for me, it's good enough for you . . ." Not because I don't want them to have better than I had, but because I don't want them to have less than I did.

"If it was good enough for me . . ." The fact is, work was *good* for me. What I want to avoid more than their disappointment now is their later inability to achieve what they want.

Put positively, I want them to know that they can provide for themselves, can dare to dream personal dreams of accomplishment, can achieve their goals, and can feel good about themselves.

Not because they always made it, but because they tried.

THE CHILDREN HAVE FREQUENT OPPORTUNITIES TO OB-
serve in their father one whose trying exceeds by a fair
margin his succeeding. This is especially true in launch-
ing myriad new TV programs.

One of the projects I've been developing this fall is
a series of TV mini-programs, two minutes each, designed to support parents in their daily life with children. At Patti's suggestion, she and I signed up for a
popular course in parenting so that I could observe
more carefully the kinds of concerns a variety of other
parents expressed.

As a research project, it was a bust. I am incapable,
it seems, of sustaining much objective distance in
that kind of give-and-take. As a result, I learned very
little about what was on their minds—but quite a bit
about changing my own.

# RIGHT TO BE WRONG— PART II

I MIGHT JUST AS WELL START WITH THE BOTTOM LINE: Alison now has her ears pierced.

Yes, I recall rather clearly putting to paper some contrary sentiments, the general tenor of which was "over my dead body." And since I have not mastered the art of posthumous writing, then some other kind of metamorphosis must have occurred.

It has.

Or, perhaps better, I changed.

Because it's mostly my fault, or responsibility, depending on how I feel about it at the moment. I had really pretty much settled the question with Alison long since, and she had wrought a few practiced phrases to interpret to her friends the kind of man she had for a father, who would not let her do what they did. She was resigned to her unperforated state, and I was nourished by the assertion of my idiosyncrasy. It felt good —almost "right"—to cut a swath wider than one's own person, even if it rolled somewhat arbitrarily over the personal desires of others.

Then I opened up the question one more time. Not with Alison, though, but with a group of parents with whom we had been meeting weekly, trying to make some sense out of parenting.

Now these people were no radical commune swingers. They were mostly polite, church-going, child-loving folks like us, who would respect a father's desire not to see his daughter mutilated for life.

Or so I thought.

They weren't even understanding. Of me, that is.

"It's her body, not yours."

"I didn't realize you had such a blind spot."

"You wouldn't put up with her telling you what kind of jewelry to wear."

I couldn't believe my ears. Had Alison gotten to all these people? How had she done it? Here they were, these thirty-five- and forty-year-olds pelting me with the same nuggets my twelve-year-old had been slinging (albeit with diminished hope of scoring, these past months). I was astonished.

Had they no feelings for me? For my years of conditioning? For my pet prejudice? For common civility, since we were gathered in *my* living room?

None.

The evening ended an eon later, with them trickling out the door shrugging into their overcoats and me mumbling numb courtesies.

Now, it is not my style to make decisions by taking a poll of my peers. Or certainly not to follow the *majority* opinion expressed therein. But it was ominously clear that a re-evaluation of my position was in order.

But how could I just give up something I so profoundly believed in? Why I had even written a loving chapter to memorialize my prejudice, and in the process had come to love it all the more. How could I face myself, if I became unfaithful to so dear a part of me?

By finding a better part, I guess.

So I went looking for it. I plowed back through those memories of Fresno, California—but with a different purpose this time: not to savor them; not to reinforce the residue of conditioning; not to bolster my idiosyncrasy.

This time I was looking for release. I wanted freedom for Alison. And I wanted change for her father, so he wouldn't be thought square.

But I really didn't want to change the private me. Not the me who lived those days, and for whom the preservation of those old feelings is an affirmation of my roots and my personal history. I didn't want to lose that part of me. Everything else changes so fast, so irreversibly. Can't I keep at least a few markers to trace where I've been?

A serious sadness seeped through me. I don't generally lack the courage to grow and change, I thought to myself, but is everything perishable?

I didn't know what would happen when I took my high school yearbook off the shelf. The issue was no longer whether Alison would get her ears pierced. Of course, she could, and would. But I needed a way to assimilate the fitness of it, to make my decision an affirmation instead of a default.

I carried my yearbook into the living room where Alison was reading and asked her to join me in scanning it. "Oh, Dad!" she exclaimed in her best good-humored sarcasm, "I thought you'd never ask. . . . Oh, Dad . . . your high school *yearbook*. . . . Wait'll the other kids hear about this!"

But she's no dummy. She had heard through the

grapevine that I had been worked over pretty well by the other parents, and she must have intuited that this yearbook exercise had something to do with the resolution of the pierced ears question. So we turned together to page 18 of the 1954 Fresno High School *Owl*, a rack of senior portraits. There, in the center of the page, right between Dahlgren and Darby, was a nice young kid named Daley.

He had hair about a quarter of an inch long.

I felt a wry smile wrinkle clear through me, and I said to Alison, "See these other kids with the long hair —like mine is now? When I was your age, they were the hoods. The bad guys. And see the way my hair was cut? Just like the crooks and con men who ran the White House for Nixon."

The following week she got her ears pierced. Since I didn't want some gypsy with a safety pin doing the job, I had to lend her a few extra dollars to cover our pediatrician's fee. Usually, we never lend the kids money. They save until they have enough. But this felt different—a way of saying I supported what she was doing.

I felt good about the decision, about changing my mind, about everything—until she came home with her ears pierced.

Then I felt sick.

I smiled and nodded and listened as she described the process to me. And I hated myself. A silent scream caromed around inside me. You dumb sonofabitch! Why didn't you stick to your guns?! You never should have changed your mind. . . . Now you'll never be able to look at her again without feeling this way, and that's a whole lot worse for her than having a father with irksome prejudices.

The harangue went on, because the feelings went on. I was truly sorry I had changed my mind. It must have lasted two weeks. Then it went away.

By then I knew I love this girl with the pierced ears more than I loved my past.

ALISON IS ONE OF THOSE PEOPLE WHO IS EASY TO LOVE for what she shows you of herself. There is a lot to her, and she lets you in on much of it.

Shannon is, as you may sense by now, quite different. She is more a poem, withholding more than she reveals, yet suggesting realms of incubating promise for both poet and beholder.

# CAUGHT IN THE MIDDLE

## *or*

## *MAKING THE MOST OF HAND-ME-DOWN PRECEDENTS*

NEWS TRAVELS FAST IN OUR HOUSE, ESPECIALLY WHEN borne on the exuberance of a twelve-year-old whose father has just reversed an adamant stand against pierced ears. And so, in a twinkling sibling synapse, our ten-year-old daughter knew it.

Shannon didn't say anything that day, though. She is like that. Sensitive, she no doubt recognized that her father was still somewhat in shock and an ill-timed question might be upsetting.

As her own birthday in March approached, however, Shannon asked me if she could pierce her ears.

My answer came so quickly she startled a bit, like a surprised fawn: "Of course, honey." She then tossed a quick little smile of satisfaction that said "Thanks, Pop" and was gone.

I doubt that Shannon will pierce her ears. Not now, or in the future. And I am virtually certain she had not the least intention of doing so when she asked me that question.

She was asking another question entirely.

Shannon wanted to know if the trail the eldest child has blazed on this issue was permanent, or whether the underbrush of paternal caprice would choke it off before younger siblings could travel that way. Once she had her answer, she slipped off silently into that quiet private place where middle children live.

And that's what this chapter is about—the world of the middle child.

The temptation, of course, was to go another way—and to talk about the trail-blazing function of older children. But that's *always* the temptation, to talk about the older one, or about the youngest. It is fully symptomatic of the life of a middle child that the struggles of the older and the antics of the younger eclipse their visibility.

It is also symptomatic that, after my having written more than a dozen and a half chapters of this book, this is the first to revolve around a quite remarkable human being named Shannon.

Curious, how we develop these systems in families whereby we silently negotiate roles and relative prominence. And curious, too, how each makes of his or her place the kind of nesting ground required to hatch who they will be.

Shannon's nest is just off the beaten path, and some wondrous things incubate there. The sorry part is how rarely I peer in. It almost requires the absence of the others before I notice what's growing there.

Like the other night. Alison was visiting in Vermont, gone for the week. Jad was spending the night with a friend. Shannon was our "only child" at dinner.

"Daddy, I've been thinking. What if a doctor had tried for a long time to help someone get well, had given them all the best medicines and stuff, but they just wouldn't get better. Is it possible that person might be talking himself into being sick, somehow?"

I allowed that such a possibility did exist, and in fact had a name—psychosomatic illness.

Shannon pondered for a minute while she quietly straightened out a couple of string beans on her plate.

"I have an idea how the doctor could cure them—but I'm not sure it would be right."

"What's on your mind?"

"How about if he gave the person a pill and told him it was a sure cure, that it absolutely would cure the illness and it was impossible for them to be sick after they took it. But really it was just a pretend pill."

I just sat there, looking at her, split thoughts running one way in admiration, another way in wondering what else I'd been missing that was going through her mind.

She went on. "I just know it would work. The thing I'm not sure about is whether or not it would be right to trick somebody for their own good—or if that would really be best for them in the long run."

We talked late into that night.

And we have talked a lot more since then. And I think about her even more than I talk to her, wondering what else she's thinking about.

I remember my own early days as a middle child, when my mother was busy with the baby and my older brother was off with "the big kids." I was alone a lot, and lonely a little.

But I think now that was vitally fecund time, those hours of fantasy and rumination and calculation. There were no facts or opinions endlessly urging themselves on me, there was little energy spent on negotiating peer relationships; just a world of interior room to grow in.

One reinvents the wheel a lot in those times. But it is of small consequence to Shannon that psychosomatic medicine and placebos have been known and named by others. She is fully their peer in discovery, and in satisfaction.

And who knows what she's dreaming of today?

I'm almost reluctant to ask. I feel rather more like figuring out some comfortable ways to help her older sister and younger brother find some more of that private time, for themselves.

But I have a more protective urge about Shannon. I want her to be able to cultivate her solitude as long as it feels right to her, as long as she feels that her private time is a growing time. I no longer think of her as a "middle child," with whatever familial-sociological characteristics are supposed to follow from that.

I think more of her as Shannon.

Shortly after I finished the foregoing reflections on Shannon, I chanced by her desk and my eye was caught by some of her reflections, done none-too-neatly in a fourth-grade hand.

### Death

a quiet, black, darkness,
silence, like after a storm.
a storm *is* over—
the fight of death against life.

then—the realization that,
you're dead.
the thing you'd been dreading all your life.
but slowly you seem to wake up
slowly, layer by layer

you feel like you're in an elevator,
you feel yourself lifted,
with only a slight stirring of air
and quickly for a few fleeting moments

you see the people you loved
and everything that happened in your life
but before you know what's happening it's over.

you're there
up in the strange mysterious heaven.
a feeling of relief
and a fresh beginning spreads over you.

—SHANNON PATRICIA DALEY
1975

WE HAVE PRETTY WELL SETTLED INTO OUR HOUSEHOLD routine for the year. There has been a waning of September's constant juggling of schedules to accommodate lessons and driving responsibilities and household jobs and meetings. October has brought stability of a sort to our weekly calendar, if not to our lives. We all know what we're supposed to do, and when. I think we're going to make it once more.

Not, however, entirely spontaneously.

# "BUT I DIDN'T
LEAVE IT THERE"

*or*

## STRUGGLING TO CREATE A TEAM EFFORT
IN HOLDING THE HOUSE TOGETHER

WE SHARE HOUSEHOLD JOBS VERY WELL IN MY FAMILY.
In one of our periodic spasms of liberating sympathy
for Patti, we hit upon a way of dividing up most of the
tasks that "normally" fell to her. We distinguished between personal upkeep (bedroom, teeth, pets) and family upkeep (meals, vacuuming, yard). Each person was
assigned one family upkeep task, to be changed every
week.

So, every fifth week, we had breakfast prepared by a
five-year-old. Or dinner by a nine-year-old.

Not that you'd have done much finagling to get invited to meals at our house, but it worked. The dinner
cook was responsible for developing a shopping list for
evening meals that week, and for soliciting lists from

the breakfast and lunch cooks, and for conducting the marketing foray.

It really did work. Scurrying up and down the aisles of the A & P, the children would shout out comparisons of price and size. With their rudimentary math skills, they groped toward the best buy, struggling to stay within the fixed budget assigned for the week. A glow of pride enveloped them as they swept through the checkout line with a few cents to spare.

Since the plan was instituted a year ago, there have been some minor modifications, and we rotate jobs much less frequently. For several months now, Shannon has been on breakfasts. Alison does lunch, and I do dinner. Patti does the vacuuming and Jad the yard. We all like what we're doing better than the other jobs, and so we'll keep this pattern until someone wants relief.

We share the jobs well.

What we do not share so well is the responsibility.

Nagging is the gritty lubricant of our square-wheeled machine. Every single day of every single week of every single month, I am nagging somebody. Not to *do* their job. Everyone does the job, after a fashion.

But to do it *responsibly*.

As I write this morning, the kitchen is clean. The price of its cleanliness, however, was more than I wished to pay. It consisted of three reminders to Shannon that the breakfast dishes needed to go into the dishwasher and that the scraps of scrapple must be wiped up. Then two reminders to Alison that the milk would not survive the day unless it went back into the refrigerator, that the mustard glops on the counter would leave stains by evening, and that the bread would not be enhanced by a day-long exposure to the air.

I am no cleanliness nut, either. On a slovenly-to-fastidious scale of 1–10, you'd have to peg me about three or four. I'm capable of going months—even years—without noticing that the light transmission through our windows has been reduced by 40 percent because of smeary handprints, or that those are not tennis balls but dust balls I step over at the foot of my workbench.

I'm really concerned only about the essentials—like meals. Patti, on the other hand, would be pegged closer to eight or nine on the scale. But since she works full time, she is in no position to indulge her inclination to sanitation, and so it becomes our joint family responsibility.

I mean, joint task. Because the children just aren't responsible. They do their work, and a lot of it, but only at the price of a prod.

When do they just start *doing* it?

Perhaps in about twenty years, if they take after me. Now that I think about it, I spent a major part of my early years malingering.

Saturday morning, my father would appear for breakfast in baggy khaki shorts, an ancient polo shirt, and some nondescript old moccasins. And I knew what that meant. A day in the garden, with a few intimate indentured servants at his elbow.

I am as fond of gardening as I am of cats.

For some of the same reasons, too. My father had a preference for plants which puncture the flesh. Pyracanthas. Cactus. Holly. Roses. If there was a more lethal garden on the face of the earth, it could only have graced the grounds of the palace of the Marquis de Sade.

Our flower beds were booby-trapped with little rose twigs, overlooked when the previous year's prunings were picked up, and now hidden under leaves. Short and stout, these mace-like sections had only one or two large thorns on them, which had enjoyed a year of seasoning till every whisper of moisture had evaporated, rendering the weapon utterly devoid of any merciful pliability. When the meaty part of your knee, just below the kneecap, suddenly settled on such a spike, it hurt like hell.

Saturdays, I spent a lot of time in the bathroom.

Since my father was a keen man and no doubt understood that I had neither the incapacity of bladder, nor the infinite capacity for self-exploration, to warrant the hours I spent there, he must have thought me lacking in a sense of responsibility for the garden.

So he conscripted me, nagged me, badgered me. He taught me to hate spiked plants.

But I somehow wound up loving all the rest.

For all the time I spent hating what I was doing, there must have been some nurturing going on. Now I do make sure there are growing things in view around me, both at home and at work.

Perhaps I would do well to scrutinize my nagging, to see whether what I bother them with is likely to have a residue that matters. Since I can't just yammer at them about everything, I might just as well lay off the inevitable nuisances and concentrate on the areas where lasting values are created.

WHEN I WAS A KID, IT SEEMS LIKE WE WERE MORE EASILY conscripted for things like yard work because we spent more time just messing around, with nothing apparent to do. Nowadays, the kids' time is stuffed full of organized entertainment from dawn till well past dark.

Daylight Saving Time has just gone into hibernation for the winter. We gained an hour of sleep last night, and lost an hour of after-school daylight for months to come.

It was not an even trade.

With the children in the house early these dark November afternoons, play possibilities are limited. And when the old refrain "I don't have anything to do" is sung, it's hard to keep them from falling into our culture's most ubiquitous witlessness.

# THE TROJAN HORSE
# OF TECHNOLOGY
## *or*
## *A MAN'S HOME IS NOT A STABLE*

BY THE TIME HE HAD REACHED AGE SIX, IT WAS CLEAR
that my only son was becoming an addict.

We knew, of course, that all children are potential
addicts. Consequently we had rationed the dosage for
Jad just the way we had with his older sisters. Just a
little bit, spread out over each week. And it had worked
well for the girls.

But Jad was different. Jad was hooked.

My only son was a TV fiend.

He had the finely tuned reflex action of a chain
smoker unconsciously and unerringly going through the
practiced motions of addiction. Sidling over toward the
TV at any time of night or day, he would pull the "on"
button and begin twirling the dial—click/click/click—
even before a picture appeared. Perhaps a dozen twists
of the wrist were shot off before a program choice presented itself.

"Jad," I would call out with both reproach and menace in my voice, "you do not have any programs on now."

"I know," he would reply with the cheery nonchalance of a true addict, as though he could take or leave what he was hopelessly hooked on. "I'm just looking."

"I *know* you're just looking. That's why I called to you. Please turn it off *now*."

"Okay, okay. Don't get excited, Dad. I'm just . . ."

Now he was into his stalling phase, trying to keep me engaged in debate while he twirled the dial, getting a snip of a "fix" from each momentary image before him.

This was the time I must bark, sharply, to break through the benumbing stupor beginning to enfold him.

"JAD!" I would shout, hard enough to hurt my throat.

A sudden jolt would blast through him, in one motion snapping off the TV and yelping wounded reply: "All *right!* You don't have to yell and scare a guy half to death. Gee whiz!"

And that would end it.

Until the next time—which might be only a matter of minutes hence. Jad managed to course past the TV with remarkable frequency, only to have the little scenario rehearsed one more time.

It really was becoming a problem. Something had to be done. And thus I conspired to commit the only intentional deception I have ever wrought on my children.

I do not deceive my children lightly. But I do have very strong convictions about disciplining children's life with TV. In America they watch far too much, most of it trash. (Not all of it is junk. I have been associated for many years, both as a writer and an executive, with "Mister Rogers' Neighborhood," a television program designed to meet young children's developmental needs. The documented benefits of that program and others like it will endure for generations.)

But, by and large, I firmly believe that children's time is better spent doing almost anything else—building a fort or a Kool-Aid stand, reading, fighting, practicing piano, or throwing a boomerang, talking with an old person, exploring, being bored.

Especially, being bored.

The one thing I do not want to deprive my children of is boredom. For that's their main chance to find out what they have in them. If necessity is the mother of invention, then boredom is the mother of creativity and resourcefulness.

Those are the hours when children develop their fantasizing capacities, their cooperational skills, their contentedness with their own company.

Nothing new has yet been created on earth which wasn't first imagined. And this generation of children will be required to imagine and bring forth solutions to new problems and opportunities we cannot dream of.

Yet TV can rob them of those irreplaceable hours of boredom during which their minds can reach for new horizons.

And so, on Easter Sunday, I sabotaged our TV sets. Just like that.

It is really quite simple, once you have decided to do it. Since it is a safe assumption that no one in the family will be competent to ferret out the problem, practically any sabotage will do the job.

I just snipped the antenna wires, making tiny cuts which severed the copper but not the whole casing so they could be reconnected at will. To the naked eye, the antenna wire was fine.

But the picture was hideous.

"Must be the antenna rig," I announced with feigned gloom. "Darned things cost an arm and a leg, y'know, and they probably have to ship it clear over from Japan. Heaven only knows when we can get it replaced."

The children went bananas.

(And *that*, dear reader, is why I chose to deceive them. I'm hatchet man often enough, without adding the stigma of being the killer of TV. Who needs that kind of hassle?)

"Maybe we could borrow one," suggested Alison.

"Let's buy a new TV," Jad offered. "Or maybe a new house with a good TV antenna."

Their suggestions cascaded forth, ranging from the clever to the absurd. For a couple of kids lacking in boredom, Alison and Jad were certainly resourceful enough when it came to restoring TV service to our household.

Only Shannon kept her counsel. She was never a heavy TV watcher, and most of her aggregate hours with the set were sort of piggybacked on the viewing passions of Alison and Jad. So, too, her reaction was more derivative of theirs. After her initial shock and horror waned, she almost seemed intrigued with the idea of a TV-less home.

The next week was sheer hell. At every silent half hour interval, a child would suddenly cry out, as though wounded by an invisible lance.

"Oooooohohhh, now I'm missing 'Happy Days'!"

Half an hour later, another voice: "Ooooooohoohh, it's time for 'The Waltons' and our stupid TV is still broken!"

It was quite incredible. I began to imagine that secret agents of the networks had implanted some kind of perverse pacemaker in each of my children, timed to zap them half-hourly for life.

They were still getting zapped during the second week. But not as regularly.

And by the third week, the outcry had declined remarkably. From perhaps seventy expressions of pain in the first week and some forty or fifty the second, now we were down to fewer than ten.

During the fourth week, incredibly, neither Alison nor Jad made any comment about the loss. Only one child, Shannon, had anything to say on the subject.

In her quiet, thoughtful way, she found me alone one evening and said simply, "Daddy, I hope we never get the TV fixed. Our family is better off without it."

I agreed with her conclusion, but wanted to know how she reached it.

"Look at Jad," she offered. "When we had TV, he could barely read. Now he reads all the time."

That was true enough. In that short span of time—four weeks—he had turned to books as a prime substitute, and before the summer was over he was excitedly plowing through four or five hundred pages a week.

"And we get more time with Ali now. Before, all she had time for were her lessons and practice, homework, and then TV."

Also true. A ten-year-old can feel left out of the life and interests of a twelve-year-old; I remember the feeling well. But now there were occasional fireside games, where there used to be TV, and we all got more of Alison's time and attention.

In fact, this was true for all of us. Dimly it dawned on me, as the patterned presence of TV receded in our life as a family, that TV had controlled much of our access to one another.

If Jad had wanted—at 8:55 P.M.—a bedtime story, it was likely to be a five-minute venture. Maybe he really needed more of me that night—ten minutes, or fifteen.

But he wasn't likely to get it, because I would have been more attentive to the clock, for a scheduled TV event, than I was to the human concerns animating the people I love.

We all recognized what we had been doing. And we welcomed the restoration of people and their interests, not programs, as the prime determinants of how we spent our time together.

It is only fair, I suppose, to go no further without acknowledging the initial effects of TV-lessness on the adults in the household. For my own part, I really did not miss it. I watch TV very little except for snatches of sports, and spring TV sports are of scant interest to me.

But Patti—that's a different story. To our mutual surprise, my accomplice in this deception turned out to be a closet addict. Here she had been taking little fixes three times a day and neither of us had even noticed, let alone recognized it as a true addiction. For Patti's habit was not the prime time programming.

Patti was a news junkie.

Every morning, as she dressed, she would take a few jolts from the "Today" program, hourly and half hourly. Again in the evening, a little offhand sampling of Walter Cronkite's stuff. Then, just for good measure, one last nightcap at 11:00 P.M., to make sure nothing had happened since dinner of which she must properly take note.

What a wretched sight, seeing my own wife writhing in the agonies of withdrawal, questioning the wisdom of our sabotage, and cursing *The New York Times* for coming only once a day.

But she, too, discovered a silver lining to the beclouded tube on our TV sets. Not only did once a day prove often enough for *The New York Times* to come—there were even details of the stories beyond the headlines. Imagine! Details, to take one beyond awareness to *understanding*. It became clear that her addiction had been a hopeless kind of self-perpetuating compensation for the insufficiency of what news she saw. She knew there *must* be more to the story than she had just heard, so she waited for the next installment—which was never enough either.

But her addiction waned as well.

Months passed. Not every night was a cozy Norman Rockwell scene of the family playing Monopoly before the fire, but some were. Some, where there had been none. We got along without TV just fine. Even the one misgiving I had pondered never materialized—the children did not feel "out of it" in schoolyard conversations which, inevitably, include reactions to the latest TV episodes.

During those months, three TV events came to be so prized by all the family members that I made special arrangements to "borrow" an antenna just for the programs. And thus our horse-loving household saw all of Secretariat's Triple Crown races, each one followed by the immediate disabling of our TV set again.

Then came the fall.

And, with it, football. Now, I do enjoy watching a good football game, all the more so that Jad has become a rabid fan. What a fine thing, it seemed to me, for a young lad and his daddy to hunker down for a few hours of rooting for our favorite teams.

Besides, we had been without TV for over six months now and I felt confident the addiction was fully broken.

What I didn't know was how little time it took to reestablish it.

About three days.

That's how long the new antenna had been on "semi-permanent loan" when it was clear that Jad was hooked again. First thing in the morning or after school, on went the set. His traffic pattern began to show the old detours through the family room again, just to flick the switch and twirl the dial on the off chance that . . .

It was clear that Jad was addicted again, but it was clearer to Alison than to me. So she took me aside one day and told me what to do.

"Dad, there's a problem with Jad and the TV. He's at it all the time when you guys aren't here. I think maybe it's time that you return the antenna you . . . ah . . . 'borrowed' from the office."

She *knew!*

Not just about Jad—but about me, about the antenna, about the grand deception. For how long she had known, I have no idea. I didn't then, and I still don't today. All I know is that one child who truly enjoyed TV was willing to disable it again on behalf of her brother.

I did what she told me.

"After all," she reminded me, "you can always 'borrow' it again for something really special."

But I didn't think Saturday football games would plausibly fall into that category, and in my desperation I made a startling discovery:

Do you realize that in the same way that prime time TV programs seen on the screen depict real live actors and actresses in a studio or on location, in the very same way there are real live football players actually cavorting about stadia performing the feats—in three dimensions—seen in 2-D on the tube? It is true. I have now seen them with my own eyes, with my own children, with my own hot dog dripping mustard on my own shirt.

It's better than on TV.

Once you get used to it, that is. The first ball game we went to I found surprisingly annoying for the first five or ten minutes. I just felt sort of mildly disgruntled —disagreeably so—and decided to take a mental time-out from the game to identify the roots of the feeling.

I narrowed it down quickly to a feeling of deprivation, as though I were missing out on something. But what? Then it came to me.

No instant replay!

That's it. No showing the same play over and over and over again from six different angles, until you know it by heart, whether you want to or not. Suddenly I knew, too, that instant replays are in the same category with endless news programs: If what you're seeing is substantially less than reality, you try to make up for it by repetition ad nauseam.

Perhaps TV fare is the Chinese cooking of the mind, leaving us perennially ravenous an hour later.

Enough of that. Back to the ball game, which I henceforth reveled in for its sights and sounds, for the mob, for the *immediacy* of it all. (Immediate—i.e., no media to get between reality and me.) I even enjoyed, for the first time, the hour it took to creep, bumper-to-bumper, out of the parking lot and make the drive home.

We had a lot to talk about, too, after each of several other games remaining in the season, as I expect we will more often next fall. A family Christmas present to each other is going to be some season tickets. We may not feel like doing that every year, of course, but ordering them last fall was a good way to plan to perpetuate such immediate pleasures together.

We may even share a media pleasure or two, as well. After "borrowing" an antenna occasionally during the second six months of TV-lessness, it began to appear that no one—not even Jad—cared much about spending time that way anymore. A full year without television had let the immediate pleasures come fully into flower in all our lives, and the addiction now seems truly moribund.

And so, while the sets are functional now, nobody watches all that much anymore.

The TV may be hooked up, but we aren't.

I DO A FAIR AMOUNT OF SPEAKING, MOSTLY TALKING about children and TV. In the middle of this football season—after we discovered they do the games live, without instant replay—I went to New Orleans to do a nine-day lecture series. Patti was able to arrange a four-day weekend for herself so that she could accompany me for a gourmet tour during the first part of my stay there. We tasted everything—including 1984.

# SUPERDOME

## *or*

### *SUPERDUMB?*

UNFORGETTABLE, THAT PLACE, FOR REASONS WE NEVER anticipated. Southern hospitality anywhere below the Mason-Dixon line is fabled, of course, but a host with the resources of New Orleans can really put on the dog for visiting firepersons. Our host—a warm friend first met during our Scotland summer—outdid himself. He knew every fine eating place in the city. From breakfasts-at-Brennans to post-midnight doughnuts and coffee at Café du Monde, we didn't miss a succulent calorie anywhere. Most of them still show on me.

The one place our host took us where I didn't expect to be tempted by the cuisine was a football game at the New Orleans "Superdome," a colossal coliseum. And I wasn't. But I was knocked agog by what I found there.

Not the cavernous arena, awesome as it is—being the largest indoor volume of unobstructed space yet built by man. One does have to honor that with a genuine "Wow." But the thing that bowled me over was less a tribute to mankind's construction prowess than to our mindless cultural televisionitis.

High above the synthetic playing surface of the football field is a gigantic multi-sided screen, visible to all, on which are projected—are you ready for this?—instant replays.

Would I lie to you?

Not only do those 1984-ish screens loom over the whole people event and reduce it to two dimensions for replay; the screens also carry the plays "live."

No. Clearly, "live" is the wrong term.

Dead-but-still-kicking, perhaps.

Patti and I simply couldn't believe our eyes. Repeated observations of the crowd showed that a majority of them were watching the TV screen during the live action, ignoring the three-dimensional real players right below the screens.

Would I lie to you?

The others in our party—our host, and a former professional football player who has performed in the Superdome many times—confirmed our judgment about where the crowd was focussed. The ex-pro summed up the experience of playing in the place: an unearthly nightmare, with all human dimensions of sight and sound and interaction warped beyond recognition. (Never mind the fact that he credits the artificial surface with the career-ending damage to his legs.)

Our seats were close to the playing field, so the screen was almost directly overhead. Thus we were spared any temptation to crane our necks to look up. But for those in the upper reaches of the stadium, I suppose it's simply easier than trying to follow those increasingly remote figures down below.

In fact, the most privileged patrons of the Superdome

seem to have given up on the live game entirely and to have gone one better than the super-sized TV screens (which suffer some technical distortions).

They have, in effect, gone home to watch the game.

At half time we went aloft to ogle this hermetically sealed tiara of private boxes ringing the very uppermost reaches of the stadium. They are the glass-enclosed lounges furnished by each boxholder in his or her own version of homey sumptuousness, for entertaining guests and/or clients during the games.

But the Superdome is so huge, and these boxes are so high, you just can't see the football field from there. Well, that's not really true. You can *see* it, but it appears the size of, say, this book on the floor at your feet when you are standing erect. (I was reminded of those mile-high aerial TV shots of football taken from blimps, the purpose of which always utterly escapes me.)

I do not know whether the Superdome planners knew in advance that the most expensive seats in the house would not have a view of the proceedings. (I shudder at the quick thought that they *did*—that this is part of the whole inversion of reality.) But under any circumstances, they were not daunted.

TV, again, to the rescue.

Suspended in front of the glass wall separating the boxholders from the teeming masses is a normal TV set, like yours and mine. The denizens of these boxes—who have paid something like $25,000 for their vantage point —sit up there and watch the game on an ordinary TV.

It must be said in fairness, however, that each set is hung just *outside* their glass enclosure, in the same general expanse of space in which both the live game and the giant-screen depiction of the live game are taking place.

That has to be worth something, just in symbolic value.

This TV set carries—in sharper fidelity—the same thing that is carried on the super-screens over the playing field. But that is clearly insufficient for many of the boxholders who, cut off by glass walls from the general coliseum space and crowd, no doubt wonder from time to time what's really happening out there.

Is anybody cheering, for instance.

So most of the boxes I inspected also had a regular TV set *inside* the box, tuned not to the closed-circuit signal source feeding the outside set and the super-screen, but to a local commercial TV channel carrying the game, complete with commentary and field-level microphones keyed to transmit sounds of players and fans.

Same as what people watch at home.

It is, withal, the ultimate triumph of technique over purpose.

Would I lie to you?

But that's all right. I don't even believe it myself, and I saw it.

Live.

I HAD TO MAKE AN UNEXPECTED DETOUR THROUGH INDI-anapolis on my way home from New Orleans. Since there are no direct flights, I wound up on three different planes and passed through four different airports before I got back home.

Plenty of opportunity, you'd think, to fetch a little remembrance for the wee ones. But I'm fairly unregenerate about such things. Always have been.

# "WHAT DID YOU BRING ME?"
## or
### COMING HOME FROM A TRIP EMPTY-HANDED IS A BUMMER

FROM TIME TO TIME MY WORK HAS REQUIRED A LOT OF air travel. I sort of enjoyed it, at the outset. Somehow I felt important to blithely buy multi-hundred-dollar tickets and wing away in gigantic airliners, enjoying the ministrations of flight attendants and agents, drivers and baggage handlers.

But the part I always liked most was the return trip, when the work was done and I could begin to anticipate being reunited with my family. Settling back into my seat with a Scotch to sip and a magazine I would never get around to reading, I dreamed away the hour or two flight, savoring the moments to come.

The dream was vibrant, and stood up for many replays. It made me feel comfortable, and even more important.

The reality was something else again.

After the first great clutch of greeting, with wife and

three children all finding a part of me to encircle and squeeze, a strange ritual gradually unfolded.

Underlying the scramble to determine who would carry my bag and briefcase, there was a ripple of unrequited curiosity. The children snuffled around like eager puppies, wanting to find something. Anything.

Finally one of them would surface the question that alloyed their welcome: "What did you bring me, Daddy?"

Nothing.

Nothing at all.

I never brought them anything. I hadn't gone on that trip for the purpose of shopping for my children; I had gone to work.

And it annoyed me to have my welcome tempered by the notion that my personal return wasn't enough for them. I had to bring back some . . . some dumb thing . . . to make it complete. Why couldn't they be glad just to see *me?*

I felt even more demeaned by the vision of the kind of junk they'd likely have been thrilled with. All those airport gift shops are festooned with it: grotesque inflatable toy planes with their flabby elephantiasis, coated with a slight dulling patina of dust, hanging by a wire and turning slowly in the rush of air travelers. Anonymous stuffed animals with eyes too lifeless, plush fabric too shiny and bright, stitches stretched at the too-obvious seams. Little wooden boxes, reddish and smooth, identical in every airport save for the decal on top—a space needle in Seattle, the Golden Gate Bridge in San Francisco, the Gateway to the West arch in St. Louis, the Empire State Building or the Statue of Liberty. Business must be good in the little wooden box works of Taiwan.

No thanks to me, though.

I disdained the goods, and I rejected the notion that I needed to bring something home to the children.

Then a couple of things happened to change my mind—a little. Not that I now patronize airport gift shops; they still give me the shivers. But my children taught me what they were really looking for.

A couple of years ago while in London on business, I wrote a letter to each of my children. Two years later, those letters are still taped or tacked in a prominent spot on their bedroom walls and bulletin boards. And it's not oversight that they're still there; other artifacts have come and gone, and the letters have come down for wallpapering or painting. But they always go back up.

I think they value the letters for two reasons. First, because they give evidence that I thought about them and still cared for them even while we were an ocean apart.

And, second, because they are purely personal communications between us; they confirm our being on the same wavelength at a given moment in the time of our life together.

Toting home and puffing up a distorted vinyl toy 747 can do some of the first. I think I can acknowledge that now. It says, I thought about you while we were separated; here's the evidence. And, if the gift is uniquely appropriate to the child, it can even say, I have noticed your recent interest in airplanes, and so I brought you one.

Any child would like to know he is that carefully known. So would any adult, for that matter.

But I am still no convert to bringing home a surprise every time I travel, or even to writing a letter to my children. Because they also taught me the value of a true surprise. It happened last Christmas.

Even though there are no completely credulous believers in Santa Claus in our home any longer, Patti and I still take (and give) great pleasure in procuring stocking gifts with some care. Nothing big—but thoughtfully chosen, for the most part. A refill roll of plastic tape for a child's empty labelmaker. A new master link to fix a broken bike chain. A name plate for a bedroom door.

The children don't know exactly what "Santa" will slip into their stockings Christmas Eve, but they know they will be getting something. After all, it is Christmas. Patti and I, on the other hand, have contented ourselves to stick a couple of relatively desultory items in our own stockings, just to have something to open along with the children.

So come last Christmas Eve, we followed our usual custom. We brought our sleeping bags into the living room to spend the night, sleeping in a snug family cluster before a roaring fire. We all hung the stockings, nestled together for a little while, and reluctantly let the evening go.

After the children were asleep, Patti and I tiptoed to the hiding places to retrieve the little gifts we had squirreled away. We stuffed the children's stockings, dropped a token trinket in our own, savored the moment one last time, and slipped off to sleep.

In the morning, our stockings were overflowing with gifts. Santa had come again, while we slept, and had taken care of a pair of parents who couldn't take proper care of themselves. Sometime in the wee hours his three young conspirators had awakened one another and executed a surprise planned weeks in advance.

The torrent of feelings I had—surprise, of course, but pleasure, honor, sentimentality, pride—didn't blind me to the twinkle of satisfaction glittering around and between the three of them as they watched us.

And that moment has stayed indelibly with me, as a paradigm of gift giving. Not that it is expected, but that it is unexpected. Unpredicted. Not that it is geared to occasions, but to people. Not that it is done from duty, but from a childlike impulse to express love.

I still find traditional gift-giving occasions useful as reminders that people like to be remembered, but I also came home empty-handed from a foray to get a birthday gift for Alison this year. I told her I couldn't find anything that spoke of where we two are just now. One day I will encounter it, and both give her a gift and us a surprise.

THE FOOTBALL SEASON IS MORE THAN HALF OVER NOW, and if all the winners aren't yet confirmed, at least the also-rans know full well who they are.

In fact, some of the newness that comes with fall has faded on several fronts. Once-multicolored leaves lie uniformly brown on the ground. Once-vehement resolve to preserve lots of "family time" has faded, too, in the face of demands at work. And new teachers who seemed zingy to the kids in September have had time to show that they, too, can be fairly ordinary.

What's more, the children's interest in going to church has dwindled to the level of random curiosity. Now each week has to supply its own *raison d'être* or the show is over. Full-scale Sunday morning mutiny is always just one boring worship service away.

Fortunately, the children have been enthralled by the unique worship we engage in. So far.

I monitor their interest with an intense admixture of hope and anxiety.

# THE PERILS OF
# RIGHTEOUS WRATH

## *or*

## "JUDGE NOT, LEST YE BE JUDGED" (MATTHEW 7:1)

PERHAPS I HAD BEEN MORE FRUSTRATED ON ONE OR TWO occasions, but I couldn't remember when. And didn't want to. I expected to fully enjoy my outrage at the children's squandering a priceless learning opportunity. The situation was perfect. After all, what better justification for my high dudgeon than their inattention in *church?* Oh, the limitless fund of righteous wrath to be scooped up and flung at my quaking waifs.

The scene of the crime was worship-in-the-round, an experimental group of a dozen families which meets weekly in a comfortable lounge to worship in an informal and highly personal, interactive way. Each week a different family devises and conducts an original format for our experience together. One family might lead us in a dance interpretation of a biblical story, while another will choose to stage a mock trial on an issue of social justice. A typical "hour" of worship begins at 8:30 A.M. and ends around noon. The theme and structure change every Sunday, and only one thing holds constant—everyone in the group, from preschoolers to the elderly, is actively involved practically every minute: acting, singing, marching, cutting, painting, debating, dancing, questioning.

The only time they aren't totally engaged is when someone else talks for more than a couple of minutes in introducing an activity.

Like last Sunday.

The leaders were the youngest family in the group. Both parents were pleased and excited and nervous. Not only were they leading worship-in-the-round for the first time; they had chosen the occasion to perform and celebrate the baptism of their newborn daughter.

And so the father stood up in the center of the room to say what baptism meant to them, and what it might mean to us to participate in the service. Most of the children were sprawled on the carpet, while the adults sat next to the children or in chairs around the perimeter of the room.

He spoke for several minutes.

As he talked, I grew profoundly aware of two things. First, I was listening to the most sensitive, eloquent, simple, and yet theologically sophisticated interpretation of baptism I had ever heard.

Second, my children weren't paying him the slightest bit of attention.

Rather, they were counting the panes of glass, or daydreaming or re-tieing their shoes or cracking their knuckles or making faces to-nobody in particular.

Their seeming inattention was mildly discourteous and that was bad enough. But it also cost them a chance to learn something beautiful that was being magnifi cently taught. Such chances are too rare to squander.

I glared at them until my head ached.

Fierce thoughts of reproach ricocheted around in

my head, destroying the few words that were still finding their way into my mind. The madder I got at the kids, the less I heard. And the less I heard, the madder I got. Oh, they were really in for it now.

We were scarcely seated in the car before I let them have it. He was saying something Very Profound, I told them, and you didn't hear a word. There are times when you must be mature and at least act your age. You should have paid close atention! That was a once-in-a-lifetime opportunity! I won't tolerate your being theological ignoramuses!

My children looked at one another, slightly confused.

"What part didn't you want us to miss?" asked Alison. "When he said baptism was like the symbolism of decorating a Christmas tree?"

"Or the part just before that," Shannon asked, "when he told about how olden times people thought water had magical powers?"

Alison corrected her, big-sisterly, "It wasn't the 'olden times people,' Shannon. It was the Egyptians, before the time of Christ."

"Yeah, that was neat," Jad chimed in, "when he said about how they would kill a guy who stole the water."

Shannon continued, "I liked the part best where he told us we had to have hope ourselves before we could conduct a ritual of hope for a baby. I think that's right."

"So do I," someone added, "because . . ."

They were no longer responding to me. They simply carried on the conversation all the way home. It was a stimulating presentation. I assume they eventually covered the whole thing, although I am not in a position to judge. I had missed quite a bit of it the first time.

Because I hadn't been paying attention.

THE CHILDREN SURPRISE ME A LOT. PLEASANTLY, FOR THE most part.

One of the nicest surprises that comes my way happens when I think I'm giving a gift—the gift of time—to my children. Time *feels* like a gift when I give it, because I seem to have so little of it. I am seriously overcommitted in my work and am struggling to prune away the projects which have less meaning to me. By mid-winter I simply must terminate fully half of what I am doing, and that makes me sorry.

And grumpy.

I am facing for the first time the serious realization that I cannot do all I dream of doing. Continuing the pursuit will be costly in ways I do not care to contemplate.

And so I eke out an hour here and there, as a down payment on other, better, ways to spend my time.

Some of the best of those are one-to-one moments with Alison or Shannon or Jad.

# "SPECIAL TIMES"

## or

## MAKING/TAKING TIME TO BE A MENTOR TO AN APPRENTICE ADULT

DAYS GO BY END TO END, SEAMLESS ALMOST, AND BECOME weeks and more weeks. Or months: time flowing—and nothing happening between my children and me.

I have not talked with them, nor they with me. Neither of us is in touch with the other.

It is not silence. Just emptiness.

During those days—or is it months?—I do not feel as though I am raising my children. I feel rather as though I am just letting them grow up. And I don't like the feeling.

It's not as though they need **me** hovering over them, fathering their individuality into oblivion. Children need room to grow, and plenty of benign neglect. I try to give them both.

But this other, this empty time, is something else. I lack a sense of where they are. Not physically, necessarily (although I'm often enough ignorant of their whereabouts), but a sense of what concerns them, or what they try to master, or what shift in interests comes over them. They change, they grow, these children.

I don't want them to grow into strangers.

Trying to keep in touch at dinner time doesn't make it. The what-did-you-do-at-school method elicits only verbal as opposed to nonverbal emptiness. Each child dutifully offers some warmed-over, single-sentence morsel, devoid of protein, secure in the knowledge that no one will pursue the thought beyond the interruption which is bound to come, as remnants of dinner get passed or spilled or cleared away.

Nor is much likely to transpire in the hours after dinner, unless a pressing problem impels one of the children to lay claim to my time and attention. There's just so much else going on—homework and pet care and dishes and meetings and capture-the-flag and practicing piano/cello/violin/ballet or what have you.

So we invented "special times"—one child and one adult paired up and alone together, for a whole day, even. We just go somewhere, two of us, away from the rest of the family and the world, which might siphon off attention. It is memorable time.

Deciding what to do is as memorable as doing it.

"Shannon, you and I are overdue for a special time. What do you say—want to see the 'Nutcracker Suite'? Or how about a tour of the new sculptures on the university campus? Maybe a picnic bike-hike?"

"Uhh . . . that sounds pretty good. Any of those would be neat," she supposes without enthusiasm.

I ignore the tone, and press for a quick resolution. "Well?"

"Actually, I was wondering if . . . you'd teach me how to use your tools."

Shannon? My elfin artist? Grubbing around with my tools?

"Are you sure?" I ask, knowing she is.

She retreats, quickly, insisting "It was just an idea. I'd love to do one of those other things you said."

The subtlest, most enduring value of "special times" is on the line. Will I deflect her back onto the track of my image of her, my expectations for her? Or will we both follow her to someplace only she can lead us?

Some days I don't feel like groping along after a child's curious meanderings, preferring a more predictable and pre-packaged "good time." But this is a better time, today, because I feel up to tracking Shannon—to finding out where she's going.

"Did you just want to find out how the tools work? Or do you have a particular project you'd like to work on?"

"Are you sure you want to do that," she checks, almost coy now, "because I'd be just as happy to . . ."

I interrupt. "I'm sure."

"Neat-O! Let's fix up my cubbyhole."

Of course. That's the missing link. Not that Shannon isn't perfectly capable of wanting a short course in the use of tools, in lieu of going somewhere, for a special time. But wanting to apply them to her cubbyhole makes everything fit.

The "cubby," located behind her bedroom wall, is twenty feet long but only four feet wide and five feet feet high. It is an odd nook of space, almost like a secret. The cubbyhole was created inadvertently, two years before, when we undertook a major expansion and remodeling of our split level house. (Of the eleven originally identical houses on our cul-de-sac, the most distinctive one nowadays is the one left untouched, since the rest of us have undertaken extensive personalizations.)

I spotted this curious cranny during construction, just as they were about to wall it up. "Hold on," I said. "Just tack some Sheetrock over that space, but don't seal it up. We may want to have access to it some day."

The day had come.

Like a couple of adventurers uncovering a treasure cave, Shannon and I pried and crumbled the plasterboard from the waist-high opening. As we lifted the panel away from the opening, a barely perceptible billow of cool air rolled out across us. Standing tiptoe on Shannon's floor, we leaned into the darkness, peering fiercely to see what we now possessed.

Dimly, the contours emerged again. We were at the mid-point of the space, the floor chest high to me, with a low roof sloping away ten feet in both directions, like a sleeping loft in a mountain cabin. Plenty of space for a pair of mattresses, one on either side, with a landing in between.

Suddenly we were chattering excitedly about making it just hers. We would need to build a couple of steps, of course. And a light. No, two lights, one for each side. Paneling over the studs was a must.

"And do you suppose you could build maybe a little shelf right there, to hold my alarm clock and some things I want close?"

"Anything you say."

Shannon and I spent a fair amount of time making that space hers. She learned a little about using tools, in the process. But I learned more about her than she did about tools. About her being the one among our children with the pronounced need for a place of her own. About her willingness to forego some usual pleasure jaunts—the kind she could have told her buddies about—in order to follow more elusive, more important impulses. And I learned about how fragile those impulses are, how tenuously held, how readily subverted to adults' indifference, and yet how powerfully expressed when nourished by just a hint of affirmation and interest.

I like to think it doesn't matter much that a cabinetmaker had to finish the job, when I couldn't eventually marshal enough time to do it right. Shannon and I had some memorable hours together.

And I can hardly wait to find out what she's cooking up for our next special time.

THE PROGRESSIVE SETTING ASIDE OF SOME OF THE TOO-many projects I was involved with, coupled with the virtual elimination of TV, means more time—more interaction—with the children. When it's not annoying, it's fun.

Alison, Shannon, and now Jad are all avid readers, carting home piles of books from the library each week. And each book—each page—springs them more irretrievably into that magical world where what they find out is doubly valued for what it lures them into next. The questions propagate endlessly, and when the children sense that I am receptive they come to me with them.

Sometimes I do all right, if I remember what I'm really doing.

# WHO WANTS TO KNOW?

## *or*

## TAILORING RESPONSES TO ASKERS, NOT TO QUESTIONS

I DON'T KNOW EXACTLY HOW OLD I WAS THEN—SEVEN OR eight, probably—when I became aware that World War II necessitated the use of synthetic rubber. At least, that's about when I asked my father during Saturday breakfast what the difference was between real and synthetic rubber.

My father knew about a lot of things. He knew a dismaying amount about natural and synthetic rubber. About two hours' worth, as I recall.

While he got into the ideal agricultural and climatic conditions for growing rubber trees, I was experimenting with ways of damming and channeling the flow of egg yolk, to coat each triangle of the white equally.

Some time later, probably about the time he was well into the refinery processes of crude oil, I was on my third piece of toast. Our toaster, one of those flat-sided metal tepees with the flop-down doors, toasted one side at a time. And I had just discovered what a nice sensation it was to toast one side crispy, and butter it, but leave the other side untoasted. Even though the bread curled a bit toward the toasted side that made a nice concave surface to pack with peanut butter. With the soft, untoasted side down against my tongue, and the buttered side up to chomp down on, that was a juvenile gourmand's delight.

Dad was well into tire-molding and baking processes.

I tried doing tic-tac-toe with a tine of my fork in the dried yolk now coating my plate. But it was no fun playing against myself, so I fell to just making designs, and to building up beads of pasty yolk on the tine tips.

I learned a lot that morning.

In fact, I learned my lesson so well that I never did find out why we couldn't get tapioca during the war, or why we could get margarine but not butter. I surmised that tapioca was made up from something now needed for the war. But I knew butter came from cows and couldn't fathom why the war would keep the cows from making butter.

I was not about to ask.

And I swore to myself that when I got to be a father I would never, ever give too much answer for too little a child. Within limits, I suppose I have been faithful to that resolve. Because I have some book-learning my father didn't, I know enough about children to have a fair sense of how much—both in complexity and duration—they can take. I try to edit my answers accordingly.

But now I think that is a minor virtue.

For the more closely I listen to the children's questions, the more I conclude they don't care much about information, however well edited, even if that's apparently what they're requesting.

Data they can get from books. They want something else from me.

And so I now try to respond to askers, not to questions: Why is *this* child asking this question at this moment? Is this child after information, or understanding?

I don't do it all the time. I don't even do it most of the time. But every time I do listen to the person instead of the question, I learn a lot.

Alison's wanting to know how much money I make arose out of a particular need, different from whatever lay behind Shannon's asking the same question a year earlier. I learned something about my own needs by fathoming hers. And Shannon's wanting to know if she could pierce her ears certainly had a different objective than did Alison's pursuit of the same question. I came to love her more fully for sensing it.

Of course, I'm not quick enough to figure it all out right away. Sometimes days go by before I understand. But even when time has passed I still gain a sense of the season of growth the child is in. And, I gain a sense of how that child needs to use me, as a resource for the current season. The more I get in tune with that child's needs, the more likely I'll give an appropriate response to the next question.

The children become three-dimensional—no, four- or five-dimensional—when I begin to sense the flow of their lives behind their questions. An attic of memories becomes animated, and dramas I lived at seven, or ten, or twelve are played out with a new cast, with surprisingly fresh variations. And I become curiously renewed, as the parent-me is nourished by the child in me who is kindled in kinship with these children of mine.

But I don't suppose the child in me will ever recall what I was wishing we would buy, instead of new tires for a 1936 Packard.

As Christmas came upon us, I coincidentally had occasion to keep abreast of the trade journals in the toy industry. At work, we've been trying to decide whether we want to extend our television program activities into tangible playthings.

I read a marketing analysis which indicated that the average U. S. family would spend about $100 on Christmas presents for each child; not only that, but the average expenditure goes *up* as family income goes *down*.

The report did not say, however, whether the average expenditure per child was higher or lower depending on the number of kids in each family. My guess—based on our household—is that the more kids, the higher the per-child outlay, as each child escalates his requests according to what he thinks the others may get.

Despite our good intentions to practice benign deprivation, we still get buffeted about. This season was no exception, and now the process has swept us past the end of the year and clear into February.

# CHRISTMAS COMPETITION

## *or*

## IT IS MORE BLISSFUL TO GIVE EVEN-HANDEDLY THAN TO SEE GOD

UNTIL THE COMPETITION SET IN, OUR CHRISTMAS PLANS for the children's gifts were a model of sensitivity. Owing largely to Patti's continuing perception of their needs—as distinct from their wants—we intended to buy a few, key surprise items which would affirm and delight each of them.

(The "needs" were not to be construed as mundane necessities—the underwear, socks, and the like which we palm off as gifts from time to time. The things they need are more symbolic. They are tools which facilitate new growth. An easel and paints can be a "need.")

Alison needed a dog.

Lord knows there are a dozen other things I would rather that she felt she had to have—all inanimate. We already have a houseful of creatures presently scurrying, or hopping, or slithering, or swimming, or chirping, or barking their way through the day. They require a bewildering array of foodstuffs, and recycle them into an even more impressive array of droppings. We most assuredly did not need one more pet in the place.

But Alison did.

At age twelve-going-on-thirteen, she has been at one of those important transition times in life. It is the moment when a new focus of energy and attention can help wrap up some of the loose ends of childhood and simultaneously provide practice in adult responsibilities and procedures. When Alison began to talk about a dog of her own—a purebred canine to seriously show and breed—we remembered how important such responsibility had been to Patti at a parallel stage in her life.

So we said yes.

But the word "yes" formed itself *very* reluctantly in our minds. We knew we were stretched to the limit—beyond, often—in our ability to manage the household menagerie (including humans). There was a certain quite authentic dread of how we would cope with the added hassle—the feeding, the nagging about feeding, the pee stains, the frayed tempers about the pee stains, trips to the veterinarian and so on and on.

And on.

A dog with good bloodlines, one with championship potential, is costly beyond the hassle, though. They can command quite a few dollars, as well. And so we announced to Alison that her dog and accouterments would be her major gift for both Christmas and her birthday, in February.

That was fine with her, of course. The dream of having her own dog to show and to breed seemed special enough to count for an infinite string of gift-getting occasions. We probably could have amortized the present over every holiday clear through high school graduation, if we'd been cunning enough.

We were smitten with guilt, instead. How could we divest ourselves of all that money for Alison's dog and spend such a paltry amount on the other children?

Our guilt was fueled, of course, by a few well-timed inquiries by Shannon and Jad about factors of equity. It was no secret to them that we were combing the country for a top caliber puppy and were prepared to spend more for it than the sum of their modest requests.

How do we get into these things, anyhow?

I *know* there is no defensible correlation between what we spend on them and how completely any gift is an expression of our love for them. No correlation at all.

And yet, my control over feelings and forces like that is utterly defective, to my great anger and shame.

And so we upped the ante.

Shannon would get new pink shag carpeting for her bedroom, for Christmas. I don't remember what Jad was to get. Probably he doesn't either, which is part of the craziness of the whole exercise.

Anyhow, there we were: on the line for a mega-dollar wonder dog for Alison, who needed it to segue into adulthood; on the line for a mega-dollar carpet for Shannon, who needed it because her room is an important kind of nest for her, and because its purchase established a superficial equity in her mind and in mine; on the line for something or other for Jad, who needed it because I needed him to need it or some such nonsense.

Yeccch!

Once you get started on that kind of a wandering

from common sense, nothing good can come of it. Such a rickety structure of artificial accommodations can be felled by one freak gust.

This gust blew up from Florida, where we had finally located *the* dog for Alison, a beautiful beagle puppy with impeccable championship bloodlines. He was perfect in every respect, except one.

He cost next to nothing.

The breeder, a sensible man who loves dogs and children more than money, wanted this pup to go to someone like Alison, and so he sold us a first-class show dog for the price of a common household pet.

So much for my stupid equity scheme.

Yet the repercussions were slightly delayed. Christmas came and so did the puppy, "Copper" by name. Alison was ecstatic. Shannon's carpet came and was duly laid; it was just right for her and for her room. She, too, was ecstatic. Jad got whatever he got and loved it, no doubt.

The children were all happy.

Only the grownups displayed anything less than euphoria. Despite the fact we saved a few bucks, and Patti rekindled her earlier beagling emotions, Copper *was* a hassle to have in the house.

Our yard is unfenced and our township forbids dogs to run free. Copper must stay indoors during the day. Yet no one is home during the day to defend the furniture from his puppy gnawings, the carpets from his untrained bowels and bladder, the garbage from his ravenous pillaging.

We tried everything.

But nothing worked, except locking him in a sizable cage during our absence. That was an unsatisfactory long term solution, however, and just about the time

Alison's birthday came around in February I was preparing to build a kennel and exercise run in our backyard.

As fate would have it, that was just about the time Alison was preparing to write out a modest list of birthday gift suggestions. As became quickly apparent, the bargain basement price paid for Copper must have annulled, in her mind, the fact that Copper and accouterments were to serve as gifts for both occasions.

"What do you mean, the kennel is my birthday present?!" she demanded incredulously. "Shannon's going to get a full birthday, but her rug cost three times what Copper cost!"

I am appalled by that kind of competitive computation, and it makes me heartsick to hear one of my own children indulge in it, however natural the feeling.

I become even more heartsick when I sense my own complicity, having sought a silly "balance" of gifts.

But even though I had nurtured the equity notion, I was not about to perpetuate that thankless quagmire again. So we had a good fight.

Alison stuck to the equity line since she knew instinctively I had to justify a change in rules I had originally set.

I would like to be able to report that I said or did something insightful or winning.

Instead, I just got angry—at Alison, for being an ingrate; at Copper, for being a pain in the house; at myself, for being unable to say or do something wise.

It was Patti who put us back together.

With tears of frustration, she recalled how reluctantly we agreed to admit one more demanding creature into our home. She pointed out that we would have preferred to buy an inanimate object of virtually any price rather than that dog. Yet that dog was the *right* gift for Alison.

And so Alison re-valued Copper, according to the price we really paid. And we built the kennel and dog run, and that was her birthday present. And Copper is still more trouble than he's worth.

To me.

But he came along at just the right time for Alison, and that means he was worth the price we paid.

Now if I could only get Alison and her father to stop thinking about the price of gifts at all . . .

THE INTENDED YEAR OF THESE CHRONICLED REFLECTIONS slid blithely past New Year's, leapfrogged over February's kennel-building, and landed us on the island for another summer. It seems right, somehow, that the arbitrary symmetry of a year-long journal has been disdained by the tide of life which swept us back here, where a modest voyage would bring these writings to their proper destination.

# LETTING GO
## *or*

### BOTH FAMILIES AND FEELINGS NEED SOME ROOM TO GROW

WELL NOW, THAT'S A LITTLE MORE LIKE IT.

Captain of the ship, lord and master of all I survey. I give the orders, and everyone—even Patti—obeys without question. What power!

That's how it is when we are sailing. A kingdom for a closet czar.

Till last week, I had tasted only nibbles of power on afternoon-long sails about the bay. Heretofore the boats we chartered were day sailers, and we confined our time on the water to two or three hours on the loveliest of afternoons, gliding gracefully through Goose Rock Passage, around into Ebenecook Harbor and then out past the lighthouse on Hendricks Head. In a particularly spanking breeze, perhaps we'd venture around Lower Mark Island and the bell buoy at the edge of the ocean proper before sliding back past Five Islands to our quiet mooring in the protected waters of the Little Sheepscot.

All the while we were out, I was in charge.

In fact, something of a transformation would come over me. Where I am passive around the house, here I am all initiative and authority. Where I ignore messiness at home, aboard a boat I am fastidiousness personified; "shipshape" is no mere figure of speech to me. And where I yell at people only some of the time on terra firma, on the water I am unrestrained.

Perhaps, after the events of this past week, I will temper and harmonize some of that. If I had had some foreknowledge of the week, I probably would have avoided it. But then, I don't usually have the wits to choose what's best for me—if it's going to hurt.

Last week we went cruising. Five of us, in a twenty-two-foot sailboat equipped, after a fashion, for four. We had chartered this good little boat for our month's stay on the island, intending to use it largely for day sailing. But we couldn't resist the temptation to test its—and our—cruising capabilities on a four-day jaunt. Any reservations we might have had were swept aside by the urgings of friends who wished to cruise along with us, in their much larger boat, and by the fact that the owners of our boat had sailed for several weeks with five people aboard.

We left last Wednesday. Because our boat was smaller and therefore slower than our friends', we sailed ahead of them, calculating to rendezvous at Fisherman's Island east of Boothbay Harbor. But their departure was unexpectedly delayed, and we bobbed around a barren island, warily eyeing a massive fog bank lumber toward us, then away, then back again.

As the fog drew ever closer, I grew more tense. Our small boat was nearly as ill equipped to navigate in the fog as I am. Between us, we had one compass and an untrained crew with no applicable experience.

"If the fog gets close enough to obliterate the southern tip of Burnt Island," I told my family, "we're getting out of here. We'll cruise some other day."

But our friends reached us before the fog, and I gladly followed their big boat replete with all manner of electronic instruments. Fortunate for us they had all that gadgetry.

Within minutes, thick soft fog enveloped our boat and we were straining fiercely to see dim contours of their stern ahead. The seas began to rise, and the boats rolled dramatically. We leaned sharply forward, as though to urge our small boat closer to theirs.

For two hours of deep fog and gathering darkness, we saw nothing but the ghostly image of their boat, fading into the grey and out of it again, dropping behind a huge wave and rising to crest the next. I was determined to stay linked to them, for without them I was utterly lost.

On the whole, I thought to myself, I prefer day sailing on the bay.

Then it was over. Our course had been true, and the rocks south of New Harbor loomed ahead. In a matter of minutes we had jubilantly swung into the clear evening air of the protected anchorage and moored among the lobster boats. The tension lifted, and the evening passed like a good dream—our boats tied side-by-side, children and adults sitting around talking and eating and drinking.

And this adult asked some very earnest questions about the use of all that navigational equipment. I did not feel very competent.

Not all the tension had lifted.

Morning presented us with a sailor's vision of heaven. Brilliant deep blue skies, flat seas asparkle with the glitter of sun on the millions of wrinkles made by steady breezes. We left the harbor with visions of a once-in-a-lifetime sail.

And so it was. Cutting smoothly across Muscongus Bay, I felt like the king of the world. The boat was well trimmed; Patti was contentedly reading in the cockpit beside me; the children were variously sprawling and scrambling around the deck.

Patti saw our son tumble: "Jad's overboard!"

I whirled around just in time to see my son slip by under the surface of the water and come up astern, between our boat and the dinghy we tow behind us. I was momentarily frozen.

"Grab the dinghy, Jad!" It was Patti, cool-headed and quick.

Before I could do more than silently root for my seven-year-old, he had taken a couple of quick strokes to align himself with the dinghy, threw an arm over the side of it, and struggled against the pull of the rushing water to haul himself aboard.

Then it was over. He sat there in the dinghy, dripping, smiling, proud, and slightly oblivious to the full potential of the drama. In another minute he was back on the sailboat, changing into something dry.

I sailed very cautiously the rest of the day and thought about how ill prepared I was for such an emergency. How ill prepared we *all* were. I wondered how I would handle the next emergency.

Not all the tension had lifted.

By late afternoon, we had entered Penobscot Bay and made Tenants Harbor. The anchorage that night was as idyllic as the one before, and the next morning brought an equally lovely day. As we cleared the mouth of the small harbor, our friends headed their big boat north to keep a previous appointment and we headed our tiny one southeast, out to sea.

Our destination was Monhegan Island, seemingly well out into the ocean if your craft is but twenty-two feet long and you have been intimidated by the cruising guidebook's description of the place: beware the powerful tides sucking through the "harbor"—actually just a channel between Monhegan and neighboring Manana Island; find a permanent mooring, because your own anchor will never hold through the night; avoid the island's southern tip, where invisible currents sweep boats on the rocks; when ashore stay away from the edge of the cliffs, since the rocks crumble easily and will drop you into the waters below; above all, don't get caught in the waters at the base of the cliffs, where the surging waves create water so foamy that you are unable to swim.

A charming picture.

Gives one a bit to think about during the five-hour sail toward this awesome rock, the last land before the Gulf of Maine becomes the open Atlantic. I wished our friends were still sailing beside us, especially when a shark cruised close by. After all, they had suggested we return home via Monhegan.

But I agreed.

Now I felt foolish. With cause.

We made the passage without incident, located a strong permanent mooring, and found ourselves ashore by mid-afternoon. A hike across the island brought us to the celebrated cliffs, fully as awesome as painted, and we stared with fascination down at the fringe of beautiful, deadly turquoise foam girdling the foot of the rocks. The whole place made me fearful, and I longed for the gentler, friendlier island we call home. It seemed a long way off, and I was anxious to finish the next day's return sail without incident.

By the time we returned to the boat, it was apparent

that the weather was about to change. By nightfall, our little boat was bobbing and rolling uncomfortably. Around midnight Alison, who had been sleeping under an awning over the cockpit, hauled herself and her sleeping bag down below, soaking wet from a wind-driven downpour. She soddenly curled up on the tiny double berth with Patti and me, feeling none too cheery.

At almost any dark hour that long night, at least one other miserable person was awake to talk with. Daylight came very slowly.

And when it came, so did the fog.

Not even the intrepid lobstermen and fishermen dared venture out of the anchorage, so impenetrable was the endless wetness all around us.

I hated it. I hated the fog for keeping us from going home. I hated Monhegan Island for being so forbidding a place. I hated myself for dragging my inexperienced family crew out there.

So I yelled at them a lot.

Until finally they had enough.

Alison took the lead. "Look, Dad, let's get something straight. Every time you ask us to do something, if we don't do it right away you yell. But how can we ever figure out how to do it with you yelling?"

"That's right!" added Shannon. "You never tell us how to do it, either. Some things on a boat are complicated. You just think we can automatically do it."

"Or maybe you don't *want* us to know how," Jad charged, "so you can yell at us some more."

Maybe I don't *want* them to know how?

My God, there was some truth to that. I had never really given these people, my own family, any thorough instruction about the boats we sail.

And I suddenly knew why.

I felt ashamed. Yes, children, I thought, I will tell you what I know. I will relinquish the secret knowledge that keeps you in my thrall. I will teach you to be captains as well as crew, and I will share the helm with you. And perhaps, if I am lucky or wise enough, I will someday find more pleasure in sharing control than in prolonging your dependence on me.

The Coast Guard said the fog was not going to lift until evening—too late for us to sail—so we prepared to go ashore again. We were, by now, quite literally sick. I suspected we could find a high meadow just above the fog where we could bask in the sun and recoup our spirits.

We did better than that. As Patti and I sipped a welcome cup of hot coffee in a small restaurant, our next-door neighbor from Princeton walked in. In a matter of minutes, we were comfortably lounging in their waterfront cottage and marveling repeatedly at the coincidence of our chance meeting.

Surely some guardian angel was watching over us.

The afternoon slipped into dinner, and, with the lifting of the fog, a magnificent sunset spread before us. Clear skies stretched to the horizon, and tomorrow's sail home promised to be exhilarating.

It was all of that, and then some.

The clear weather was borne, it seems, on some extremely strong winds straight out of the northwest—the very direction in which we must travel. And the winds drove before them nasty, choppy, steep waves at very close intervals. It was the roughest water I have ever been in, and my day-old resolve to train my family had not yet yielded enough new competence to make me feel very secure.

After a hard hour of blasting into the teeth of the wind and sea, we had made less than two miles' progress, and at that rate we might not make the mainland by dark. I had had enough first-time experiences already on this trip and did not care to add nighttime navigation to the log. I asked Patti and Alison to remove the jib; we would start the engine and motor back, using the mainsail just for stability.

They slowly picked their way forward on the pitching deck until they were kneeling at the bow, which was bucking and plunging into each oncoming wave. Just as they were about to drop the jib, a particularly steep wave broke right over the bow and knocked them back. Sudden visions of their being swept overboard gripped me, but when the spray left my eyes there they were, firmly hanging on—soaked, but intact.

Quickly, they snatched in the thrashing sail, tied it down, clambered back into the cockpit and went below to dry out as best they could.

For hours yet to come, our boat would smash its way through ragged ranks of ugly waves, the small outboard engine straining to maintain the hull's momentum against the constant surging weight of the water piling into our bow. Every wave sent drenching cascades blasting across the decks and cabin, into the cockpit. Out of morbid curiosity, I counted the number of separate sheets of spray that drenched me in one sixty-second span. Thirteen, in a single minute.

There were many of those minutes, and everyone tried to help me through them. Alison came back to the cockpit to keep me wet company. Shannon called up interesting snippets of information or better-than-average riddles to amuse me. Jad asked endless questions of comparison between various sailboats, knowing my active fantasies about buying one. Patti passed us chunks of good cheddar and anything else that could be eaten soaking wet with sea water.

Hours and hours passed.

Then it was over.

We rounded the tip of Burnt Island and abruptly found ourselves in the shelter of Townsend Gut. We were now suddenly in flat glassy water, purring peacefully the last mile home while the wind and the water still ripped at the reefed-down boats in the open bay behind us.

We reached the dock at our island and a surge of warm relief coursed through me. Relief, and gratitude. This family of mine had somehow put up with me in what had not been one of my finer hours.

We sat in the cockpit and I started to tell them how I felt. How much I appreciated the way they came through when it counted. How I realized they needed to know more about what we were doing on the boat and that I needed to teach them, for lots of reasons. I had yelled a lot, but I had had cause, I said. Things can go wrong in a boat, especially in rough weather, on the kind of dangerous roller coaster ride we just had. It's important, I said, that everyone do what's necessary quickly and competently.

My words grew flat. Not feelings anymore. Just words about feelings, and rationalizations. I had told them I'd been tense, but not all the tension had lifted. There was something I wasn't saying. So I said it.

"Fathers can get scared too, you know."

And then I heard her again—the one who looked after my son on a bench in Battersea Park, now here to look after my father's son on a boat in Sheepscot Bay.

She said, "It's all right for a scared father to cry, too."

And so I did.

And my children comforted me.